LETTERS

TO

SERENA:

CONTAINING,

I. The Origin and Force of Prejudices.

II. The History of the Soul's Immortality among the Heathens.

III. The Origin of Idolatry, and Reasons of Heathenism.

As also,

IV. A Letter to a Gentleman in Holland, showing SPINOSA's System of Philosophy to be without any Principle or Foundation.

V. *Motion essential to Matter*; in Answer to some Remarks by a Noble Friend on the *Confutation of* SPINOSA.

To all which is Prefix'd,

VI. A Preface; being a Letter to a Gentleman in London, sent together with the foregoing Dissertations, and declaring the several Occasions of writing them.

By Mr. TOLAND.

Opinionum Commenta delet Dies,
Naturæ Judicia confirmat. *Cic. de Nat. Deor. l.* 2.

LONDON;

Printed for *Bernard Lintot* at the Middle-Temple Gate in *Fleet-street*. M.DCC.IV.

THE

PREFACE;

Being a Letter to a Gentleman in London, sent together with the following Dissertations, and containing the several Occasions of writing them.

1. IN all your Letters, SIR, you insinuate that considering the Place I am in, and the Company I keep, I must needs forget my Books as well as my Acquaintance;

the most shining Beautys, and the most splendid Equipages make a Figure here; besides a perpetual Concourse of Strangers, Men of the first Distinction in their own Countrys, whose Curiosity excited, and whose Fortunes enabl'd 'em to see other Men and Manners. Tho they abound with true and useful Knowledg, yet I own to you, that there's little to be found of what the mistaken World is apt to honor with the name of Learning; and tho they have variety of excellent Books, yet bookish Porers for Wisdom are the most contemptible sort of Animals among 'em. To judg of things here by Appearance, there's but one continu'd Scene of Love and Gayety among the Young and the Fair, temper'd indeed, but not interrupted by the Men of Politics and Employment. A hasty Passenger, or one that cannot produce himself into all Companys, sees no more; and knows

less

less than he did at home, by giving his Friends a wrong Account. But believe me, SIR, *I never met in any Part with choicer or more numerous Collections of Books in private Librarys, with freer Inquirers into the Series of History and the Secrets of Nature, nor with any (in a word) who better understood the Art of making Study a help to Conversation, of reading to good purpose by practising the World, of distinguishing Pedantry from Learning, and Ceremony from Civility.*

3. IN *such a Place you may imagine it must be my own fault, if I neglect those Studys, to which you know me so much addicted, and which I may rather improve than abandon by such variety of diverting Intervals. I assure you, that while I enjoy Health and Liberty, no Consideration shall be able to debar me from the use*

of good Books, wherein I am perswaded the only perfect Pleasure is to be found: for tho I love a great many other Pleasures natural to Man, and that I temperately indulge my self in all that are lawful, yet I must agree with common Experience, that in every one of them there's always a mixture of Pain, either in the Expectation, in the Enjoyment, or in the Consequences; whereas in going over an entertaining Book, the Reader tasts an absolute Satisfaction without any disturbing Allay, unmindful of the past, not sollicitous for the future, and wholly taken up with his present Happiness. I have therefore the Power and the Will to pursue my former Studys, as well as many Occasions to increase that Knowledg, which is the Ornament and Perfection of our Nature: but you are to impute the small Advances I make under such favourable Circumstances, not to

want

want of Inclination, but of Capacity.

4. *THO I have less Business than some People think, or at least report, yet when I first came hither, I did resolve to confine my self to Reading and Converse, without ever yielding to the Temptation of writing so much as a familiar Letter: but I was quickly oblig'd to take other Measures, by the repeated Desires of a Correspondent, to whom it's not in my power to deny any thing. The Person lives on this side the Sea, tho not in this Town; and, what will further mortify your Partiality, it is a fair Lady, who was pleas'd to ask my Opinion concerning the Subjects of the three first Dissertations in the Pacquet annext, and which I send to convince you that I was not quite so idle as you thought. She's Wife to a Man of conspicuous Dignity, which is all that imports you to know*

quaintance; which you kindly endeavour to excuse, tho not wholly to approve. As for observing no regular Correspondence, I believe you receiv'd Satisfaction in my last, nor are you to expect any thing more from me on that Subject: wherefore now, instead of the public News or the private Intrigues of this part of the World, I'll send you some account of my own Studys. 'Tis, I readily confess, one of the barrenest and least entertaining Themes I cou'd take; but you may thank your self for the Trouble, as I hope you'll acquit me from the Choice. And, first of all, I must frankly say, that you are very unjust to this Country, and that all your Comparisons between foggy Air and cloudy Understandings, between slow Motions and dull Conceptions, between immense Wilds and Marshes and indigested Imaginations or immethodical Common-places, are of our Sex use to be, who are not cultivated and polisht by Conversation or Letters; and that the Wives and Daughters of such Peasants have generally more Wit and Cunning, a greater share of Breeding and Sagacity? Whether the Exclusion of Women from Learning be the Effect of inveterate Custom, or proceeds from Design in the Men, shall be no Inquiry of mine: but if a Woman once in her Life happens to pry into Books, and that upon this she grows troublesom, affected, or ridiculous (as 'tis a thousand to one she does not) what a clutter do we make about this matter, how ready are we to improve it against their natural Genius, and what Triumphs are we decreeing to the Superiority of our own Understandings? Whereas, God knows, this is nothing at all to the purpose, or at most but the same thing with the Impertinence, Pride, and Pedantry of those Men,

who

the most shining Beautys, and the most splendid Equipages make a Figure here; besides a perpetual Concourse of Strangers, Men of the first Distinction in their own Countrys, whose Curiosity excited, and whose Fortunes enabl'd 'em to see other Men and Manners. Tho they abound with true and useful Knowledg, yet I own to you, that there's little to be found of what the mistaken World is apt to honor with the name of Learning; and tho they have variety of excellent Books, yet bookish Porers for Wisdom are the most contemptible sort of Animals among 'em. To judg of things here by Appearance, there's but one continu'd Scene of Love and Gayety among the Young and the Fair, temper'd indeed, but not interrupted by the Men of Politics and Employment. A hasty Passenger, or one that cannot produce himself into all Companys, sees no more; and knows

less

got ſome intire Volumes, which I recommended to your Library, containing nothing but the Lives of ſuch Women, among the Antients and the Moderns, as became famous in their own Time, and deſerv'd to have their Names tranſmitted to Poſterity, for their admirable Writings in Philoſophy, Divinity, Morality, and Hiſtory, in Verſe and Proſe, as well as for their approv'd Skill in Painting, in Muſick, and in all the other Arts and Sciences, in the Conduct of formidable VVars, and the Adminiſtration of Civil Affairs, no leſs than in private Oeconomy. DIOGENES LAERTIUS *dedicates to a Lady the Hiſtory of the Opinions as well as the Lives of the antient Philoſophers; and therefore we muſt ſuppoſe that ſhe underſtood their ſeveral Syſtems, many of 'em extremely intricate and abſtruſe, eſpecially thoſe in which ſhe moſt delighted, the Philoſophys of* PLATO *and* EPICURUS.

Monſieur

of good Books, wherein I am persuaded the only perfect Pleasure is to be found: for tho I love a great many other Pleasures natural to Man, and that I temperately indulge my self in all that are lawful, yet I must agree with common Experience, that in every one of them there's always a mixture of Pain, either in the Expectation, in the Enjoyment, or in the Consequences; whereas in going over an entertaining Book, the Reader tasts an absolute Satisfaction without any disturbing Allay, unmindful of the past, not sollicitous for the future, and wholly taken up with his present Happiness. I have therefore the Power and the Will to pursue my former Studys, as well as many Occasions to increase that Knowledg, which is the Ornament and Perfection of our Nature: but you are to impute the small Advances I make under such favourable Circumstances, not to

want

want of Inclination, but of Capacity.

4. *THO I have less Business than some People think, or at least report, yet when I first came hither, I did resolve to confine my self to Reading and Converse, without ever yielding to the Temptation of writing so much as a familiar Letter: but I was quickly oblig'd to take other Measures, by the repeated Desires of a Correspondent, to whom it's not in my power to deny any thing. The Person lives on this side the Sea, tho not in this Town; and, what will further mortify your Partiality, it is a fair Lady, who was pleas'd to ask my Opinion concerning the Subjects of the three first Dissertations in the Pacquet annext, and which I send to convince you that I was not quite so idle as you thought. She's Wife to a Man of conspicuous Dignity, which is all that imports you to know*

at present of her Person.

5. NOW do I see the inmost Thoughts of your Soul, as well as if I had the managing of all its Weights and Springs, or had the very forming of your Brain. You may remember how often I took the part of the other Sex against your Prejudices rather than your Judgment. I was conscious, it's true, of the Goodness of my Cause; but, without Vanity, I cou'd defend a worse against such Arguments, as were only drawn from the habitual Discourse of your Companions, from the ordinary bad Education of Women, or from the famous Ladys of that place where you happen'd to be first bred, and with whom you had a more intimate Acquaintance, than with any of a better Character, either since or before. How often was I forc'd to describe to you what rude, unmannerly, ignorant, and rough-hewn Monsters, those

of

VVars in Germany, Flanders, Spain, and the Indies: so (what seems to be yet a weightier Task) she keeps such an even Balance among the several contending Partys at home, that they are not able, according to their unnatural Dispositions, to oppress or devour one another; and even such as oppose her just Title in favor of a pretended Brother, find her as merciful in her Lenity to their Persons, as prudent in preventing their pernicious Designs. She has given sufficient Proofs that she will not be influenc'd by the Clamors of Bigots from any Quarter, as well knowing 'em to be the restless Firebrands of Society, and the Disturbers of the public Tranquillity, under pretence of having greater Zeal than others for Religion, while they only push forward their own particular Piques and Designs, tho under the false color of advancing God's Cause or the Church. Nevertheless she generously endeavours

who are only Smatterers in Learning, superficial Readers of Books, the sworn Heralds of Authors and Editions, Collectors of hard or high-sounding Words and crabbed Phrases, eager Hunters after Rules and Etymologys, or mere Scholars, and therefore mere Asses. I won't repeat what I demonstrated to you (for I thought it worth the Pains) about the Parity of the intellectual Organs in both Sexes, and that what puts 'em both on the same foot in Discourse of ordinary Business (which is deny'd by no body) makes 'em equally capable of all Improvements, had they but equally the same Advantages of Education, Travel, Company, and the Management of Affairs.

6. I MIGHT *dispense with the Trouble of alledging Reasons, where Experience is so express of my side; and 'tis not likely that you have forgot*

got some intire Volumes, which I recommended to your Library, containing nothing but the Lives of such Women, among the Antients and the Moderns, as became famous in their own Time, and deserv'd to have their Names transmitted to Posterity, for their admirable Writings in Philosophy, Divinity, Morality, and History, in Verse and Prose, as well as for their approv'd Skill in Painting, in Musick, and in all the other Arts and Sciences, in the Conduct of formidable VVars, and the Administration of Civil Affairs, no less than in private Oeconomy. DIOGENES LAERTIUS dedicates to a Lady the History of the Opinions as well as the Lives of the antient Philosophers; and therefore we must suppose that she understood their several Systems, many of 'em extremely intricate and abstruse, especially those in which she most delighted, the Philosophys of PLATO and EPICURUS.

Monsieur MENAGE *has written a whole Book of the Female Philosophers; inscrib'd to a Woman now alive, the Celebrated Madam* DACIER, *Daughter to the great Philologist* TANAQUIL FABER. *All the Learned World has done Justice to her excellent Works, and no body questions but she's one of the best Critics of our Time in the Greek and Latin Authors, of which the ample Pension settl'd on her by the French King is truly the weakest Argument, considering some others that are in his Pay. I cou'd write a Volume to you my self of such as I know to be in several Parts of Europe, without recalling from the Dead the Pythagoric Ladys of antient Italy. And among divers others in England (where nevertheless they are scarce enough) you may find a Lady not personally known to me, who is absolute Mistriss of the most abstracted Speculations in the Metaphysics, and who*

with

Stile with the rest. This has bin the laudable Method of the Antients, notwithstanding the Moderns have so strangely perplex'd their Readers with the odd manner of inserting their Authoritys: nor did ever any Person pretend that a Roman Lady of good Sense cou'd not read CICERO *of* Human Dutys, *or his Dialogues about* Divination, *because he has artfully wrought into his own Text and Words, so many Passages of the Greek Writers; whereas no Woman on Earth (and very few Men) can make any thing of* SELDEN *or* SALMASIUS, *without being tir'd and disgusted, which cou'd not fail, even had they written in the vulgar Languages. To say that Ladys ought not to be troubl'd with Authority in Reasoning, is not only to say that they are unreasonable Creatures, but also that the Scripture must never be quoted to 'em in Religion; because the Men will not let them*

gave hopes to the Papists of her Favor at the first, that she might afterwards (as she did) with the greater Security establish the Protestant Religion on an unshaken Foundation? Thus she became in a small time the Terror of her Enemys, the Darling of her Subjects, the Support of her Allys, and fill'd all Europe then with Envy and Admiration, as she has since done the whole World with her Name. At this very instant, Queen ANNE, *who graces the same Throne, and who proposes* ELIZABETH *for her Pattern, abundantly shows what a Lady is capable to do. For as she yields to no Prince whatsoever for the Administration of common Justice in her Dominions, in maintaining most powerful Fleets by Sea and numerous Armys by Land, in heading the Grand Alliance of so many different Nations and Persuasions against the Tyranny of France, and providing fit Supplys for the*

Wars

give such an Education to your Daughters (if ever you have any) as to be a leading Example to others: for the Practice of one Man of Fortune, Birth, and Reputation, has often gone very far towards reforming a whole Country. As for others, 'tis no matter if they still believe SERENA *a Romantic Name, like the Marchioness of Monsieur de* FONTENELLES *in his* Plurality of Worlds: *for they'll be so just however to acknowledg, that if I had the making of a Woman according to my own Fancy, she shou'd be quite another thing from those vain, giddy, affected, pratling, and gawdy things, who are as cheap as they are common, and who, as they are nothing but Outside themselves, value nothing but Outside in others; being Strangers to all good Qualitys, void of solid Vertue and true Merit; fit only for an hour's Diversion or Amuzement, but not for the principal De-*

light and indiſſoluble Society of Life. This is no more a Reflection on the Women, than on the generality of the Men, whoſe Foppery, Singularity, Pride, Ignorance, and Intemperance, muſt ſet 'em at leaſt on an equal bottom with the other Sex. Nor ought this Conſideration to heighten your Averſion, but your Caution, ſince being none of thoſe Men, you may reaſonably expect your match among the Women.

10. *BUT leaving the Ladys for this time, I muſt prepare you a little,* SIR, *for reading the Letters annext, by telling you the ſeveral Occaſions of writing them. The Subject of the firſt Letter is* The Origin and Force of Prejudices, *not from their phyſical, but their moral Cauſes. The Occaſion was my ſhowing to* SERENA *the following Paſſage of* CICERO.

Neither

* Neither Parents (*says he*) or Nurſe, or Schoolmaſter, or Poet, or Playhouſe depraves our Senſes, nor can the Conſent of the Multitude miſlead them: but all ſorts of Traps are laid to ſeduce our Underſtandings, either by thoſe whom I juſt now mention'd, who when they receive us tender and ignorant, infect and bend us as they pleaſe; or elſe by that Pleaſure which lies ſo deeply rooted in every one of our Senſes, the pretended Follower of Good, but the real Mother of all Evils, corrupted by whoſe Allurements, we do not ſufficiently diſtinguiſh thoſe

* Senſus noſtros non Parens, non Nutrix, non Magiſter, non Poeta, non Scena depravat, non multitudinis Conſenſus abducit: at vero Animis omnes tenduntur Inſidiæ, vel ab iis quos modo enumeravi, qui teneros & rudes cum acceperunt, inficiunt & flectunt ut volunt; vel ab ea, quæ penitus in omni ſenſu implicata inſidet, imitatrix Boni voluptas, Malorum autem mater omnium,

things that are good by Nature, because they want this Softness and Titillation. *Admiring the masterly Strength, and yet natural Easiness of these Words, she own'd to me, that after discovering many Prejudices to be really such, yet she did not find her self perfectly cur'd of their Influence and frequent Returns. VVherefore she demanded my Opinion of this matter in VVriting, which I perform'd in as brief a manner as I cou'd, taking that very Passage for my Text; showing the successive Growth and Increase of Prejudices thro every step of our Lives, and proving that all the Men in the VVorld are join'd in the same Conspiracy to deprave the Reason of every individual Person. I have drawn as lively a Picture as I cou'd in little, of the Pre-*

---

cujus Blanditiis corrupti quæ natura bona sunt, quia dulcedine hac & scabie carent, non cernimus satis. *De Leg. lib.* 1.

judices

Stile with the rest. This has bin the laudable Method of the Antients, notwithstanding the Moderns have so strangely perplex'd their Readers with the odd manner of inserting their Authoritys: nor did ever any Person pretend that a Roman Lady of good Sense cou'd not read CICERO Of Human Dutys, *or his Dialogues about* Divination, *because he has artfully wrought into his own Text and Words, so many Passages of the Greek Writers; whereas no Woman on Earth (and very few Men) can make any thing of* SELDEN *or* SALMASIUS, *without being tir'd and disgusted, which cou'd not fail, even had they written in the vulgar Languages. To say that Ladys ought not to be troubl'd with Authority in Reasoning, is not only to say that they are unreasonable Creatures, but also that the Scripture must never be quoted to 'em in Religion; because the Men will not let them*

a French Translation of his PHÆDO, *which I recommended to her, and my answering that his Sense was pretty well represented, tho his Elegance far from being exprest; she wonder'd that the reading of that Book cou'd add any Force to* CATO'*s Resolution of laying violent hands on himself, to avoid falling under the Usurpation of* CÆSAR; *and much more that it cou'd so transport* CLEOMBROTUS *of Ambracia as to precipitate himself into the Sea, the sooner to arrive at that happy State therein describ'd: acknowledging that she found little cogent Evidence, and a world of precarious Suppositions, throughout that whole tedious Dialogue. I told her that Divine Authority was the surest Anchor of our Hope, and the best if not the only Demonstration of the Soul's Immortality. I added, that it was not strange to find this Opinion doubted or deny'd by many of the Heathens, and made a*

matter

give such an Education to your Daughters (if ever you have any) as to be a leading Example to others: for the Practice of one Man of Fortune, Birth, and Reputation, has often gone very far towards reforming a whole Country. As for others, 'tis no matter if they still believe SERENA *a Romantic Name, like the Marchioness of Monsieur de* FONTENELLES *in his* Plurality of Worlds: *for they'll be so just however to acknowledg, that if I had the making of a Woman according to my own Fancy, she shou'd be quite another thing from those vain, giddy, affected, pratling, and gawdy things, who are as cheap as they are common, and who, as they are nothing but Outside themselves, value nothing but Outside in others; being Strangers to all good Qualitys, void of solid Vertue and true Merit; fit only for an hour's Diversion or Amuzement, but not for the principal De-*

the Soul's Immortality, all that Assent is vanish'd. *She was surpriz'd to hear me talk of a Time when this Opinion begun among the Heathens, as if like other Notions it had its proper Authors, Favorers, or Opposers, all which I roundly affirm'd to her, and that withal I wou'd show her the gradual Progress of it thro all the Parts of the Earth then known, together with the true Original of the Poetical Fables concerning the Elysian Fields, the Rivers, Judges, Gates, and Ferryman of Hell, of Souls being disquieted for want of orderly Burial, and manifest Proofs that the antient Egyptians were the genuine Fountains of all Learning and Religion to the Heathen World. All this I have endeavour'd to make out, I will not say by the best Authoritys that ever were, but by the best in the*

marum cœpi cogitare, Assensio omnis illa elabitur. *Tusc. Quæst. lib.* 1.

most

most antient Books we have remaining; for in these cases Suppositions ought to go for nothing, and therefore when we say that such or such were the first that taught Astronomy, that built Temples, that practis'd Magick, we do not mean absolutely the first (for in so many Ages who cou'd be certain of that?) but the first that can be prov'd on Record so to have done; and thus I wou'd be understood whenever I express my self in that manner. I have in this Letter likewise prov'd, that the Opinion of the Soul's Immortality had not its beginning from the Philosophers, as making such an Inference from the Spontaneous Motions, Reasoning, or Speech of Men; but, on the contrary, I have shown this Notion among the Heathens to have bin first taken up by the Mob, popular Traditions often becoming the Doctrins of Philosophers, who strive to support by good Reasons what the others begun with none

or

things that are good by Nature, because they want this Softness and Titillation. *Admiring the masterly Strength, and yet natural Easiness of these Words, she own'd to me, that after discovering many Prejudices to be really such, yet she did not find her self perfectly cur'd of their Influence and frequent Returns. Wherefore she demanded my Opinion of this matter in Writing, which I perform'd in as brief a manner as I cou'd, taking that very Passage for my Text; showing the successive Growth and Increase of Prejudices thro every step of our Lives, and proving that all the Men in the World are join'd in the same Conspiracy to deprave the Reason of every individual Person. I have drawn as lively a Picture as I cou'd in little, of the Pre-*

---

cujus Blanditiis corrupti quæ natura bona sunt, quia dulcedine hac & scabie carent, non cernimus satis. *De Leg. lib.* 1.

judices

Priests, and *Altars*, their *Feasts*, and *Sacrifices*; of *Images*, *Statues*, and *Tutelary Powers*; of *Ghosts*, *Specters*, *Oracles*, *Magick*, and *Judiciary Astrology*; with the *Reasons* how *People* came to imagine that *Heaven* (or the *Palace of the Good*) was over their *Heads*, and that *Hell* (or the *Prison of the Wicked*) was under their *Feet*; why they look up when they pray, and several other things of this nature, for which it's generally imagin'd no account can be given besides *Custom*, or that in the *Abyss* of *Time*, and under the *Ruins* of proper *Monuments*, such *Originals* are irrecoverably bury'd. *Reasons* are likewise given in this *Letter* for the principal of the *Heathen Rites*, the odd *Descriptions* they have made of their *Deitys*, the ungodlike *Historys* they relate of their *Actions*, and other *Particularitys* which have bin long regarded as the *Fictions* of *Poets*, or the *Extravagancys* of human *Imagination*,

but

a French Translation of his PHÆDO, *which I recommended to her, and my answering that his Sense was pretty well represented, tho his Elegance far from being exprest; she wonder'd that the reading of that Book cou'd add any Force to* CATO's *Resolution of laying violent hands on himself, to avoid falling under the Usurpation of* CÆSAR; *and much more that it cou'd so transport* CLEOMBROTUS *of Ambracia as to precipitate himself into the Sea, the sooner to arrive at that happy State therein describ'd: acknowledging that she found little cogent Evidence, and a world of precarious Suppositions, throughout that whole tedious Dialogue. I told her that Divine Authority was the surest Anchor of our Hope, and the best if not the only Demonstration of the Soul's Immortality. I added, that it was not strange to find this Opinion doubted or deny'd by many of the Heathens, and made a*

matter

is not an Argument therefore that I have no more Reasons or Authoritys left to defend what may be reckon'd dangerous Paradoxes, by such as are mortally afraid if they are led but one step out of the common Road, tho but to make their way shorter and safer, or to walk upon Carpet Downs, instead of wandring guideless thro a Wilderness, over Lakes and Morasses, among dreadful Rocks and Precipices.

13. *YOU'll wonder, I believe, that I shou'd differ so much both about the Origin and Progress of Idolatry, with one whose Book on this very Subject I have so lately recommended to you under an advantageous Character; I mean the most faithful and laborious Antiquary* ANTONY VANDALE, *principal Physician to the City of Harlem. My Opinion of that Book is still the same, only that (as I then told you) instead of the* Origin and Progress of Idolatry, *I think it ought to have been intitul'd,*

A compleat Collection of the most antient Heathen, Jewish, and Christian Superstitions: *for these things are in that Book very accurately describ'd, but little said of their Origin, or nothing contrary to my Authoritys, except what I have confuted about the Worship of the Celestial Bodys; and the Progress of Idolatry from Chaldea to Syria and other Parts of Asia, particularly to Ionia, thence to Greece, and so on, barely suppos'd, but not offer'd to be prov'd, as may be seen in the second and third Chapters of the first Dissertation, where the Subject is indeed but incidentally hinted. Nor do I question but that learned Gentleman will prefer good Authority, tho not commonly taken notice of, to a vulgar Error, tho generally approv'd.* Mr. Vandale's *History of the Heathen Oracles you have already perus'd with great Satisfaction. He has lately publish'd eleven Dissertations relating chiefly to the Sacred Functions of the Heathens, wherein from*

Medals,

most antient Books we have remaining; *for in these cases Suppositions ought to go for nothing*, *and therefore when we say that such or such were the first that taught Astronomy, that built Temples, that practis'd Magick, we do not mean absolutely the first* (*for in so many Ages who cou'd be certain of that?*) *but the first that can be prov'd on Record so to have done*; *and thus I wou'd be understood whenever I express my self in that manner. I have in this Letter likewise prov'd, that the Opinion of the Soul's Immortality had not its beginning from the Philosophers, as making such an Inference from the Spontaneous Motions, Reasoning, or Speech of Men*; *but, on the contrary, I have shown this Notion among the Heathens to have bin first taken up by the Mob, popular Traditions often becoming the Doctrins of Philosophers, who strive to support by good Reasons what the others begun with none*

or

or very bad ones. *If what I have alledg'd be found to be true, it first confutes those who commonly suppose that the Heathens had learnt the Soul's Immortality from the Jews; and secondly the Opinion which Dr.* COWARD *has espous'd,* * *That* the separate Existence of Human Souls proceeded from the Heathen Philosophers and no others; *tho when I wrote that Letter I did not know there was any such Book in the world as the Doctor's, which I have but lately seen, and found nothing in it to my purpose.*

12. *IN the third Letter written likewise to* SERENA, *and at her own Desire, you'll find* The Origin of Idolatry, *explain'd after a very different manner from what is commonly receiv'd. There also you may read the first Causes of the Heathen Temples,*

* Grand Essay, p. 105.

Priests,

Priests, and Altars, their Feasts, and Sacrifices; of Images, Statues, and Tutelary Powers; of Ghosts, Specters, Oracles, Magick, and Judiciary Astrology; with the Reasons how People came to imagine that Heaven (or the Palace of the Good) was over their Heads, and that Hell (or the Prison of the Wicked) was under their Feet; why they look up when they pray, and several other things of this nature, for which it's generally imagin'd no account can be given besides Custom, or that in the Abyss of Time, and under the Ruins of proper Monuments, such Originals are irrecoverably bury'd. Reasons are likewise given in this Letter for the principal of the Heathen Rites, the odd Descriptions they have made of their Deitys, the ungodlike Historys they relate of their Actions, and other Particularitys which have bin long regarded as the Fictions of Poets, or the Extravagancys of human Imagination,

but

but no way to be probably reduc'd to the Exactness of History. And last of all is explain'd the threefold Division of the Heathen Theology into Natural, Civil, and Poetical, with the Allegorical Interpretation of their Mysterys, and a Parallel of their Practices with the Corruptions of Christianity; whereby it appears that in all Ages Superstition is actually the same, however the Names of it may vary. This third is the longest of all the Letters, but you'll think it impossible that in so short a one any Satisfaction can be given concerning so many different Subjects as I have already nam'd, not to insist on what I have not time to mention: and therefore you are to suppose that I don't empty common places here, and deliver all that may be said on each of these Heads (which I have bin far from doing) but only all that's strictly necessary to make 'em very certain, easy, and intelligible to a Lady, and consequently to all Capacitys. This is not an Argument therefore that I have no more Reasons or Authoritys left to defend what may be reckon'd dangerous Paradoxes, by such as are mortally afraid if they are led but one step out of the common Road, tho but to make their way shorter and safer, or to walk upon Carpet Downs, instead of wandring guideless thro a Wilderness, over Lakes and Morasses, among dreadful Rocks and Precipices.

13. *YOU'll wonder, I believe, that I shou'd differ so much both about the Origin and Progress of Idolatry, with one whose Book on this very Subject I have so lately recommended to you under an advantageous Character; I mean the most faithful and laborious Antiquary* ANTONY VANDALE, *principal Physician to the City of Harlem. My Opinion of that Book is still the same, only that (as I then told you) instead of the* Origin and Progress of Idolatry, *I think it ought to have been intitul'd,*

A compleat Collection of the most antient Heathen, Jewish, and Christian Superstitions: *for these things are in that Book very accurately describ'd, but little said of their Origin, or nothing contrary to my Authoritys, except what I have confuted about the Worship of the Celestial Bodys; and the Progress of Idolatry from Chaldea to Syria and other Parts of Asia, particularly to Ionia, thence to Greece, and so on, barely suppos'd, but not offer'd to be prov'd, as may be seen in the second and third Chapters of the first Dissertation, where the Subject is indeed but incidentally hinted. Nor do I question but that learned Gentleman will prefer good Authority, tho not commonly taken notice of, to a vulgar Error, tho generally approv'd. Mr.* VANDALE's *History of the Heathen Oracles you have already perus'd with great Satisfaction. He has lately publish'd eleven Dissertations relating chiefly to the Sacred Functions of the Heathens, wherein from Medals,*

Medals, Inscriptions, and Passages of Authors, vast Discoverys are made in Antiquity. He has at present in the Press a Confutation of the pretended ARISTEAS, *and consequently the History of the Greek Translation of the Old Testament, falsly attributed to the seventy Interpreters. In the same Volume he treats of the antient Rites of Purification and Regeneration, as Washings, Sprinklings, Immersions, by Water, by Blood, and the like; whence we are to expect many curious Circumstances relating to Christian Baptism, deliver'd not only with the greatest Freedom, but also with the utmost Fairness: for tho Mr.* VANDALE *be by Profession a Mennonist, or (as we term them) an Anabaptist, yet he's one of the most passionate Lovers of Truth, as well as of his Friends, that I ever knew; of a large Soul notwithstanding his narrow Fortune, and of nobler Thoughts than to be a Bigot to any thing against plain Reason or Authority.*

14. *I HAVE written other Letters to* SERENA, *and concerning matters much more curious; but not having yet transcrib'd 'em fair, I send you instead of them two Philosophical Letters, written to Gentlemen altogether unknown to you. The first, being the fourth in the Pacquet, was sent to an excessive Admirer of* SPINOSA, *one wholly addicted to his Principles, and reputed the best of any to understand his System. After having disputed together at several times on several Heads, I told him once, en passant, that the whole Fabrick of that Philosophy was without any solid Foundation; of which he laying immediate hold, wou'd never let me be quiet, till, getting leisure enough in a lovely Country Retirement, I wrote this Letter. Being a Person of extraordinary Candor, he freely acknowledg'd* SPINO-

SA

SA *to be defective in that point, and consequently in all that depended on it; tho he had never observ'd so much before, and some other Spinosists show'd the same Ingenuity. But a Gentleman, no less illustrious for his excellent Learning than his noble Family, having got a sight of what they stil'd the* Confutation of SPINOSA, *and which they handed one to another, he bestow'd many Commendations (not fit for me to repeat) on that part of the Letter which directly regarded that Philosopher: but exprest his Dislike of the latter part, wherein I declar'd my own Opinion, that* Motion is essential to Matter no less than Extension, *and that Matter neither ever was nor ever can be a sluggish, dead, and inactive Lump, or in a State of absolute Repose. To the several Objections he was pleas'd to make, I return'd distinct Answers in the second Letter, which is the fifth and last in*

Letter I. nish'd to find that any shou'd call the Truth of 'em in question; as it will more evidently appear from the following Reflections.

4. WE are presently after our Birth deliver'd to Nurses, ignorant Women of the meanest Vulgar, who infuse into us their Errors with their Milk, frightning us into quiet with the menaces of Rawhead and Bloody-bones, Bugglebows and Bullbeggars. And lest we shou'd be lost by wandring abroad, or drop into Wells or Rivers, they terrify us with storys of Spirits and Hobgoblins, making us believe that all lonesome places are haunted, and that the invisible Powers are principally active and mischievous in the night-time. What is thus invented at the beginning to keep Children under Government (a Government that indeed makes 'em miserable Slaves ever after) is believ'd by them in good earnest when they grow older, whereby the whole Generation and Country comes to be persuaded of it at last, and this to such a degree, that many People (otherwise prudent enough) dare not sleep alone in a Chamber, nor travel but by Day-light, much less have they the courage to enter

into

into empty Houſes or Churches. Letter I.

5. FROM our Nurſes we are brought home, where we are ſtill put into worſe hands among idle and ignorant Servants, whoſe chiefeſt Entertainments are Diſcourſes of Fairys, Elves, Witchcrafts, walking Ghoſts, Fortune-telling, conſulting Aſtrologers, or ſuch other chimerical Doings; delighting to fright and delude one another, not ſeldom to carry on their private Intrigues: which things, however intended, never fail to make fatal impreſſions on the Children: and for the moſt part our Parents are not wiſer.

6. THEN we are ſent out to School, where all the Youth come equally infected from home, and hear of nothing there but Dæmons, Nymphs, Genii, Satyrs, Fauns, Apparitions, Prophecys, Transformations, and other ſtupendous Miracles. We tell all our ſtorys over again among our ſelves; and what may be conceal'd from a Child in a prudent Family, he's ſure to hear of it at School, where ſo many Children are brought together, not to improve one another (which cannot be ſuppos'd of ſuch Converſation) but to communicate their

Letter I. mutual Miſtakes and vicious Habits, to grow the more idle, and to meet with bad Examples. We greedily devour the Poets, Orators, and Mythologiſts, committing great Extracts of their Fictions to our memory, being ſurpriz'd and gain'd by the Charms of their Stile, Numbers, and Compoſition; whereby it comes to paſs that we ſwallow the Poiſon of their Errors with inexpreſſible Pleaſure, and lay a large Foundation for future Credulity, inſenſibly acquiring a Diſpoſition for hearing things rare and wonderful, to imagin we believe what we only dread or deſire, to think when we are but puzzl'd that we are convinc'd, and to ſwallow what we cannot comprehend.

7. WE are made little wiſer, tho much more vain and conceited in the Univerſitys, eſpecially abroad, where the Profeſſors (right or wrong) muſt accommodate all things to the Laws and the Religion of the Country: or, if they ſteal ſometimes into the Liberty of Philoſophizing, they generally run into Extremes, either making us truſt too little or too much to our Senſes, or amuſing us with illuſory Abſtractions, and Subtiltys which refine the Subject

out of our View, reducing it at last to mere nothing. The University is the most fertile Nursery of Prejudices, whereof the greatest is, that we think there to learn every thing, when in reality we are taught nothing; only we talk by Rote with mighty assurance the precarious Notions of our Systems, which if deny'd by another, we have not a word further to say out of our common Road, nor any Arguments left, to satisfy the Opposer or our selves. But our comfort is, that we know as much as our Masters, who affect to speak a barbarous Jargon which commonly has no Signification; and the main Art that fits their Disciples to take their Degrees, is to treat of very ordinary Matters in very extraordinary Terms. Yet this dos not render them half so insupportable to People of Sense, as their formal Stiffness and Pedantry, their perpetual Itch of Dispute and Contradiction. I purposely forbear saying any thing of the Advantage commonly taken there from the Inexperience of the Youth (who must naturally rely on the Judgment of their Teachers) to ingage 'em betimes to different Partys and Factions, to Sourness, Censoriousness, and Bigotry: for, in one word, there Letter I.

Letter I. is ſcarce any thing learnt at the Univerſity, but what a man muſt forget, if he would be underſtood, or not appear ridiculous and troubleſome, when he comes into other Company.

8. BUT as if all this were not enough to corrupt our Underſtandings, there are certain Perſons hir'd and ſet apart in moſt Communitys of the World, not to undeceive, but to retain the reſt of the People in their Miſtakes. This will be counted a hard Saying, but it cannot concern the Orthodox Clergy: and of other Prieſts what can there be more certain, ſince 'tis for this very reaſon they are counted Heterodox? The ſtrange things and amazing ſtorys we have read or heard (if of any Concern to a particular Religion) are daily confirm'd to us by the Preacher from the Pulpit, where all he ſays is taken for Truth by the greateſt part of the Auditory, no body having the liberty to contradict him, and he giving out his own Conceits for the very Oracles of God. Tho every Sect will deny this of its peculiar Doctrines (and that we know it, SERENA, to be falſe of the Reform'd Religion which we profeſs) yet the reſt affirm it with unde-

niable Arguments of one another; for it is impossible they shou'd be all or above one of 'em in the right, which is a Demonstration that the rest, being the bulk of Mankind, are retain'd in their Mistakes by their Priests. And nevertheless the very Doubts about the Joys of Heaven and the Torments of Hell, are enough to procure Authority for their infinite Contradictions: so strong are the Impressions of Hope and Fear, which yet are ever founded in Ignorance! Letter I.

9. WHEN we come abroad into the World, we find all those Errors to be in so high a Credit, that every one is gaz'd on as a Monster, who is out of this universal Mode: or if by some lucky chance we shou'd happen to be undeceiv'd, yet the prevailing Power of Interest will make us hypocritically (or, if you please, prudently) to pretend the contrary, for fear of losing our Fortunes, Quiet, Reputation, or Lives. This confirms others in their Prejudices by our example, as much as if we were deceiv'd our selves; for knowing nothing of our Minds but by our outward Actions, which appear so like their own, they judg us to be of the

Letter I.

the same Persuasion. Besides, that to maintain we are in the Right, while others are in the Wrong, will be interpreted such an Affront to all other People, as a Man wou'd not venture to be guilty of who knows Mankind, and is resolv'd to lead an easy Life far from the Noise, and Crowd, and Hurry of the World.

10. THOSE who are more in love with the Bustle of the Publick, or more under a Necessity to endure it, generally betake themselves to some Profession. This indispensably engages 'em to many Prejudices in favor of their particular Calling, which if all of 'em do not always believe, yet they find it their interest that others shou'd do so, to gain with them the greater Credit, Reputation, and Authority. CATO the Censor wonder'd, that when one Augur met another, they did not laugh at the Simplicity of those who believ'd their Divinations; and if they had done so among themselves (as we know from History they often did) yet they wou'd never the sooner expose the Craft of their Order to the People, who thought 'em the infallible News-mongers of Heaven, and who paid 'em so well for their

their Intelligence. Hence not only every Profeſſion, but alſo every Rank of Men, have their particular Language, which is thought by others to contain very extraordinary Matters, much above the common Capacity or Comprehenſion. The Nobility, Country-Gentlemen, Jockys, and Beaus, have as well their ſeveral Cants (tho not ſo barbarous) as the Divines, the Lawyers, Phyſicians, and Philoſophers. Except the few wiſe and cunning, all the reſt are really perſuaded that they are far greater Men than ſuch as are ignorant of their Terms; and I have many times ſeen a Hunter as much deſpiſe the good Senſe of thoſe who did not underſtand his noiſy Jargon, as an Aſtrologer very proud of illuminating the credulous Mob with that vile Stuff, which he did not ſo much as underſtand himſelf. In moſt Profeſſions (eſpecially in thoſe they repute Mechanick) the Members are ſworn not to diſcover the Myſtery of their Trade, which very Notion of Myſtery makes others imagin that there's ſomething extraordinary in very trivial matters thus artfully diſguiz'd; and your Myſterys of State (tho not to be pry'd into by vulgar Eyes, but to be admir'd with Veneration) are ſome-

times

Letter I. times as airy and imaginary, as slight and ridiculous as any others.

11. BUT no sort of Prejudices stick closer to us, or are harder to be eradicated, than those of the Society wherein we live and had our Education. This holds equally true of their civil Customs and religious Rites, of their Notions and Practices. We cannot easily be brought to believe that our Ancestors were mostly in the wrong, much less that those with whom we daily converse have so little ground for many of their Actions: especially since we are as apt to love, or to admire the Opinions of Men as we do their Persons, and that we are bred in the same Persuasion as well as they. On the contrary likewise, we frequently hate the Opinion for the sake of the Person, and not less frequently the Person for the sake of his Opinion; commonly for no better reason, than that we were differently bred, and accustom'd to think that one who errs in his Notions cannot be right in his Practice. Thus the Body of the People in all Places of the World do greedily imbibe whatever they are taught to imitate or to respect from their Infancy, and without further Evidence

dence are ready to die for the Truth of it in old Age; which is to become properly Martyrs to a Habit, but not to Religion or Truth, unless by mere Accident. Nay, Custom (which is not unfitly call'd a second Nature) has imprest such a Stamp on the very Language of the Society, that what is deliver'd in these or those Words, tho never so contradictory or abstruse, passes ordinarily for current Truth: but change your Terms, or use the Expressions of any other Party, and then if you speak Oracles, whatever you say is reputed false, or at best suspected. And indeed it cannot well be otherwise, since these Prejudices of all others must never be examin'd. You may reason your self (for example) into what Religion you please; but, pray, what Religion will permit you to reason your self out of it? I know some of 'em profess to allow a Liberty of examining, but their Proceedings not seldom show their want of Sincerity: for let any of their Doctrines be call'd in doubt or deny'd after such an Examination, and the Person that dos it will pass his time very ill. If he's not put to Death, sent into Banishment, depriv'd of his Employments, fin'd, or excommunicated, according

Letter I. cording as his Church has more or less Power; yet the least he may expect, is to be abhorr'd and shun'd by the other Members of the Society (a thing in all People's power) which every Man has not Fortitude enough to bear for the sake of the greatest Truths; and the very Dearness of Acquaintance has often retain'd Men of admirable Understanding, in the external Profession of the most absurd and ridiculous Errors.

12. ADD to all this our own Fears and Vanity; our Ignorance of Things past, the Uncertainty of the present Time, and our sollicitous Curiosity about what's to come; our Precipitation in judging, our Inconsiderateness in assenting, and want of due Suspension in examining: which makes us not only be carry'd away by vulgar Errors in our Practice, to be misled by our Senses as well as by our Appetites, and to take numberless Falsitys for demonstrated Truths in matters of Speculation; but likewise to be unjust to the Merit of others, to confound the Innocent with the Guilty, and generally to prefer the latter. And, as our Prejudices govern us, 'tis next to impossible we should ever truly discern who is the innocent

innocent or guilty Person, who has got the better or the worse of any Cause; since our first Question is not what a Man has done or how, but who or whence he is? being ready to approve or condemn, to read over his Book or to throw it away, according to the Faction or Party he espouses. This surely is neither fair nor manly dealing: and I hope nobody will pretend that it is the way to discover Truth, no more than to continue stedfast in the Profession of it; since it's hard to conceive (for example) by what means a Man can quit the Alcoran if he must never read the Bible; or if a Mahometan ought to read the Bible, I see no reason a Christian shou'd fear to read the Alcoran; which is as true of all the Books in the World. It were superfluous to speak any thing more at large of such common Places as our predominant Passions, the Contagion of the consenting Multitude, or the Authority of our most mighty Master, the irresistible Tyrant Custom, which equally rules over Princes, Priests, and People.

13. AFTER these Observations we may perceive the perillous Condition of every particular Man, and how impossible

Letter I. possible it appears for him to escape Infection, to obtain or to preserve his Liberty; since all the other men of the World are agreed in the same Conspiracy to deceive him. But tho a Person exempt from Prejudices seems in his outward Circumstances to have little advantage over others; yet the cultivating of his Reason will be the chief Study of his Life, when on the one hand he considers that nothing can equal his inward Quiet and Joy, seeing almost all the rest of his kind ever groveling in the dark, lost in inextricable Mazes, agitated with innumerable Doubts, tormented with perpetual Fears, and not sure to find any End of their Misery even in Death: while, on the other hand, he himself is wholly secur'd by a right use of his Understanding against all these vain Dreams and terrible Phantoms, content with what he already knows, and pleas'd with new Discoverys, without thinking himself concern'd in things inscrutable; not led like a Beast by Authority or Passion, but giving Law to his own Actions as a free and reasonable Man.

Letter I.

14. I AM as ſenſible as any in the World, SERENA, how little you need that I ſhou'd further inlarge on this Subject, you having already ſo much Knowledg and ſo few Prejudices, reaſoning ſo exactly, thinking ſo nicely, and ſpeaking ſo juſtly. Nor is it for your Inſtruction (I confeſs) that I have written now at your Deſire, but to ſhow you how much we agree in our Opinions; tho I am ready to acknowledg that you exceed moſt men as well as my ſelf in Quickneſs of Underſtanding, as you do all your own Sex by your many excellent Qualitys. In the matter of Prejudices, you ſee that at leaſt you are not in a worſe ſtate than other Perſons; or if your Circumſtances are better (as I'm ſure they are) nevertheleſs you muſt be content with the inward Pleaſure and Satisfaction of your own Mind, and not expect the Applauſe of the Publick, which wou'd rather expoſe you to Diſgrace or Danger, than do Juſtice to your incomparable Virtues. But this ought not to hinder your injoying the Happineſs of free Diſcourſe with any Perſons worthy of this Honor, whom you ſhall find to have as much Judgment and Diſ-

Letter I. cretion in reasoning, as I have Zeal and Sincerity in professing my self, MADAM, to be your most faithful humble Servant.

LETTER

LETTER II.

The History of the Soul's Immortality among the Heathens.

IF the best Religion ought to be distinguish'd by the Purity and Integrity of its Morals, as well as by the Truth and Usefulness of its Doctrins, I am not acquainted with any body more sincerely pious than you, MADAM; which is a Testimony that all those, who have the Happiness to be acquainted with you, will readily grant to your Virtue. You have no Doubts, I'm certain, about the Soul's Immortality; and Christianity affords the best, the clearest Demonstration for it, even the Revelation of God himself. But you have often admir'd, you say, how the Heathens came by the

Letter II. the Discovery of this Truth, since they had no such Revelation from Heaven, and that what is so confidently said of their learning it from the antient Books of the Jews, may be as easily deny'd as affirm'd; besides that it is altogether groundless, no such thing plainly appearing in these Books themselves, tho it be manifest from the Pentateuch and the Series of other History, that many Nations had their several Religions and Governments long before the Law was deliver'd to the Israelites. The same holds as true of the pretended Preaching of ABRAHAM, and of the Tradition of the Sons of NOAH; these being as destitute of any Evidence from matter of Fact, as in their Circumstances utterly improbable. To have therefore the pleasure, MADAM, of doing a Thing which you signify will be very agreeable to you, I shall lay this Subject before you as it appears to my self, not from Conjectures and Suppositions, which give no body any real Conviction, however they may silence or amuse; but I shall argue from unbiass'd Reasons, and the greatest Consent of antient Writers.

2. TO

Letter II.

2. TO Persons less knowing and unprejudic'd than SERENA, it wou'd sound strange perhaps to hear me speak of the Soul's Immortality, as of an Opinion, which, like some others in Philosophy, had a Beginning at a certain time, or from a certain Author who was the Inventor thereof, and which was favour'd or oppos'd as Peoples Persuasion, Interest, or Inclination led 'em. But so it was among the Heathens, whatever you may think of the matter; and I have sometimes consider'd with astonishment the weakness of those, who, contrary to their own Experience, seem'd afraid to acknowledg so much: as if the nature of the thing cou'd suffer any detriment from the Errors of others about it; or as if the Heathens had not entertain'd as extravagant Fancys about the very Being of God, and all the other Articles of our Religion, which no body takes to be any Argument against the Truth of them.

3. NOW tho the Egyptian Priests, the Chaldæan Magi, and the Indian Brachmans have disputed among themselves about the Honor of this In-

vention (no less than those of Harlem and Mentz about the beginning of Printing, and those of China and Europe about the Origin of Artillery as well as of Printing, and other Nations about other Arts or Opinions) yet it is expresly assented by ARISTOTLE,[a] and agreed by the generality of Writers as an uncontroverted Truth, that the most antient Greek Philosophers did not dream of any Principle or actuating Spirit in the Universe it self, no more than in any of the Parts thereof: but explain'd all the Phænomena of Nature by Matter and local Motion, Levity and Gravity, or the like; and rejected all that the Poets said of the Gods, Dæmons, Souls, Ghosts, Heaven, Hell, Visions, Prophecys, and Miracles, as Fables invented at pleasure, and Fictions to divert their Readers. After THALES, ANAXIMANDER, ANAXIMENES, and others had thus taught the Universe to be infinite, and Matter to be eternal, tho the Forms thereof were changeable, comes ANAXAGORAS (as it is unanimously own'd

[a] Τῶν δὲ πρώτων φιλοσοφησάντων οἱ πλεῖστοι τὰς ἐν ὕλης εἴδει μόνας ᾠήθησαν ἀρχὰς εἶναι πάντων. Metaph. l. 1.

by

by almost all Authors Heathen or Christian) and to this Matter adds another Principle, which he call'd the MIND, as the Mover and Disposer of the same: whereupon from so curious, so new, and strange an Invention he was sirnam'd * the MIND, some deriding and others admiring him for this Notion. We shall presently show how he came by this Discovery, the most of those that preceded him made infinite Matter the Principle of all things. 'Tis true that THALES maintain'd Matter to be essentially Water, as ANAXIMENES affirm'd it to be Air; and that by various Rarefactions and Condensations all things were form'd out of these Elements, and resolv'd into them again: but the meaning of both is, that the Particles of Matter are extremely subtil and in perpetual motion like Air or

---

* Aristot. Metaph. l. 1. Plato in Phædone. Cic. de Nat. Deor. l. 1. Diogen. Laert. in Anaxag. Plutarch. in Pericle, & in placit. Philos. l. 1. Tertul. de Anima. Clem. Alex. Stromat. l. 2. Eused. de Præp. Evang. l. 14. August. de Civ. Dei, l. 8. Themist. Orat. 19. Etiam Proclus, Simplicius, cum multis aliis, tam Gentilibus quam Christianis.

* Diogen. Laert. in Anaxag. Suidas in Anaxagora. Plutarch. in Pericle.

Letter II. Water; from which Motion, and the Infinity of the Universe, the whole Tribe of Philosophers (as we said just now) accounted for all the Phænomena of Nature, till ANAXAGORAS added the moving and ordering Mind.

4. ONE wou'd think that a Person, who deserv'd so well of the Greeks, shou'd have met with sutable Rewards and Applause; but whether it be that the other Philosophers envy'd him, or that they wish'd there was no Spirit, or that he did not sufficiently answer their Objections, or whatever were the reason, 'tis certain that he was unfortunate in his Reputation at that time and ever since, having bin very ill us'd by all Partys, for no cause that I can see, but that he did not fully come up to any of them. Some assert that he did not understand the corpuscular Philosophy, and that he espous'd the Opinion of the separate Mind (for he was not the Author of it) to save himself the labor of understanding Mechanicks, of making long Deductions and accurate Observations, or prying into the Nature of Things. And as a Confirmation of this, they tell you that in other Matters his Imagination

was very groſs, witneſs his [1] teaching that the Sun was little bigger than the Peninſul of Peloponneſus; that the Earth was flat, and not round; that the Firmament was made of Stones, which were kept from falling by their ſwift Rotation; that in Generation the Males came from the Mother's right Side, and the Females from her left; that Snow was black; and that the Particles of all things, as of Blood, or Bones, or Gold, or Milk, were already form'd and exiſtent from Eternity, but that they conſtituted Blood, or Gold, Black or Green, as it happen'd that a ſufficient Number of them were brought together into one Body, ſo as greatly to ſurpaſs the Particles of any other ſort, which Opinion the Greeks expreſs by the Word *Homœomeria*. They further [2] laught at him for leaving his Grounds to the diſcretion of his Sheep, that he might be the more at leiſure for the Study of Aſtronomy, in which his Syſtem of the Sun and the Stones of the Firmament ſhows he was a wonder- Letter II.

[1] Vide Diog. Laert. in Anaxagora, & ad eum Annotatores.
[2] Diogen. Laert. in Anaxagora, &c.

ful

LETTER III.

ful Proficient; they blam'd him for neglecting what was necessary and profitable in Life, and giving himself up to speculative, abstruse, and remote Considerations, which are wholly useless and uncertain; and said that he deservedly wanted Bread in his old Age, having bin in danger of starving without the assistance of his Scholar PERICLES. Those who believ'd a divine intelligent Being, counted him a mungrel Philosopher between themselves and those of the Ionick Sect, and were angry with him for not employing his ordering Mind on every occasion; for, as often as he cou'd without it, he explain'd all the Phænomena of Nature by the Action and Reaction of Bodys on one another. PLATO (in his *Phædo*) introduces SOCRATES charging him with this very matter, and showing no small contempt for his Books. For the same reason he was not counted Orthodox by some Fathers of the Christian Church, notwithstanding his adding Spirit to Matter; and IRENÆUS (in his second Book against Heresys) dos not only call him irreligious, but

* Lib. 2. de Hæres.

also

and in precise terms an Atheist, and says that he was so stil'd by others. CLEMENS ALEXANDRINUS bears very hard upon him with Puns, which I shall here render word for word. [1]ANAXAGORAS, says he, *was the first who added Mind to things: but he did not preserve the Dignity of the efficient Cause, describing certain mindless Vortexes, together with a Mindlesness and Inaction of the Mind.* And ARISTOTLE compares him to a Poet that brings off his Hero with a Miracle, when no natural Cause can save him: for he affirms that [2]ANAXAGORAS *makes use of the Mind as of a Machine in the Formation of the World; and produces it only, when he doubts by what Cause it necessarily exists: but in other matters, he assigns any other Cause of the things which are made rather than the Mind.* However, there wanted not those among the Antients and Moderns who entertain'd a more favorable

Letter II.

[1] Επει και Αναξαγορας πρωτος επεστησε τον Νουν τοις πραγμασιν; αλλ' ουδ' ουτος ετηρησε την αξιαν την ποιητικην, δινας τινας ανοητους αναζωγραφων, συν τη του Νου απραξια τε και ανοια. Stromat. l. 2.

[2] Αναξαγορας τε γαρ μηχανη χρηται τω Νω προς την κοσμοποιιαν; και οταν απορηση δια τιν' αιτιαν εξ αναγκης εστι, τοτε ελκει αυτον: εν δε τοις αλλοις, παντα μαλλον αιτιαται των γινομενων η νουν. Metaph. l. 1.

Opinion

Letter II. Opinion of him, and the great Dr. BURNET (in his [1] Archæology) says that his Sirname of the Mind is far more honorable than those of Africanus and Asiaticus: nor did ANAXAGORAS fail of setting a just Value on his own Worth; for after his Exile (whether for Atheism in ungodding the Planets, or for Treason in conspiring with PERICLES) when some body told him that he was depriv'd of the Athenians, he immediately answer'd, [2] *not I of them, but they of me*.

5. PHERECYDES of the Island Syrus, as we are inform'd by [3] CICERO and others, was the first among the Greek Philosophers that committed the Immortality of human Souls to writing: for tho THALES is said to have bin of the same [4] Opinion, yet he publish'd nothing; and MAXIMUS TYRIUS

---

[1] L. 1. c. 10.

[2] Diogenes Laertius in Anaxagora; *ȣ μενιν, αλλα εκεινοι εμȣ*.

[3] Credo equidem etiam alios; sed (quod Litteris extet) Pherecydes Syrius primum dixit Animos Hominum esse sempiternos. Hanc Opinionem Discipulus ejus Pythagoras maxime confirmavit. *Tusc. Quæst. l. 1.*

[4] *Ενιοι δε και αυτον πρωτον ειπειν φασιν αθανατȣς τας ψυχας, ων εστι χοιριλος ο ποιητης.* Diogen. Laert. in Thalete.

(in

(in his twenty eighth Dissertation) affirms with CICERO that PYTHAGORAS *the Samian*, the Disciple of PHERECYDES, [1] *was the first among the Greeks who durst openly maintain that the Body only dy'd, but that the Soul was immortal, neither subject to Age nor Corruption, and that it existed before it came hither.* You see, it was so great an Innovation, that he was reckon'd a bold Man, who had Courage enough to vent it. Afterwards PLATO and the rest greedily imbrac'd this Doctrine; and we know how widely the Grecians cou'd spread it by their numberless Colonys in Asia, in Italy, in Sicily, in Gaule, and other Parts of the World, as well as by their Poets, Orators, Historians, and Philosophers, whose Works were so much admir'd by other Nations for their Subtlity, Politeness, and Learning.

Letter II.

6. BUT the next Question is, whence ANAXAGORAS and his Followers (who pretended to no divine Revelations) borrow'd this Invention.

---

[1] Πυθαγορας δε ὁ Σαμιος πρωτος εν τοις Ἑλλησιν ετολμησεν ειπειν· ὁτι αυτῳ το μεν σωμα τεθνηξεται, ἡ δε ψυχη αναπτασα οιχησεται αθανης και αγηρως, και γαρ ειναι αυτην πριν ἡκειν δευρο.

Letter II.

It is evident from antient Monuments that he and the other Philosophers of his side, with the Poets and Mythologists, learnt it partly from the Magi, when the Persians transported their Arms into Greece, and partly from the Priests of Egypt when they travel'd for Knowledg into that Country. THALES had his Philosophy of the Egyptian Priests. PLATO was in Egypt a long time, he has a great many of the Egyptian Doctrins in his Works, and is acknowledg'd by all to have learnt of * them and of their Disciple PYTHAGORAS as well as of the Persian Magi, whatever he has deliver'd about the Immortality of the Soul, the different Mansions of the Just and Unjust in a future State, the Expiations of Crimes, the Lakes and Rivers, the Meadows, Caves, and Monsters of

---

* Diogen. Laert. in Thalete. Clem. Alexand. Strom. l. 1. Euseb. de Præpar. Evangel. l. 10. Joseph. l. 1. contra Ap.

* Diod. Sic. l. 1. Cicero l. 5. de Finibus. Lib. de Senectute. Tusc. Quæst. l. 1. Aristot. Metaph. l. 1. Diog. Laert. in Platone. Quintilian. lib. 1. Clem. Alexandria. in Admonit. ad Gent. Valer. Max. l. 8. Philostrat. vit. Appollon. lib. 1. Hieronymus lib. 2. Ep. 1. ad Paulinam. Lactant. lib. 4. cum multis aliis.

Hell,

Hell. [a] PYTHAGORAS, one of the greatest Travellers in the World, convers'd with the Chaldæan Magi, the Indian Gymnosophists, and particularly with the Egyptian Priests and Prophets, suffering himself to be circumcis'd that he might be admitted to hear the secret Doctrins of the latter, which they wou'd not communicate to him without this Condition. I will not here insist on the Poets, as ORPHEUS, HOMER, or any other of the most antient, who yet are all confest to have borrow'd their Fictions from the Egyptians, as may be seen in the first Book of [b] DIODORUS SICULUS. ANAXAGORAS was first taught by the Magi, having bin twenty years of Age at the Expedition of XERXES, and (as [c] DIONYSIUS PHALEREUS relates) he begun to philosophize in Athens at those Years. He was a Hearer of ANAXIMENES, and (as THEODORET and AMMIANUS MAR-

Letter II.

---

[a] Herodot. in Thalia. Diod. Sic. l. 1. Cicero de Finibus l. 5. Plin. Hist. Nat. l. 36. etiam lib. 25. Diogen. Laert. in Pythag. Isocrat. in laude Busiridis, & alii passim.

[b] Clem. Alex. Theodoret. in Serm. contra Græcos.

[c] Diog. Laert. in Anaxagora.

CELLINUS

Letter II.

CELLINUS inform us) had travel'd likewise into [1] Egypt; so that we plainly perceive whence he had his Notion of the ordering Mind. The Greeks learnt several things of the Magi in those Days, which afterwards inspir'd others with the Desire of going into those Parts for perfecting their Knowledg.

7. BUT the great Doubt still remains, who were the first Inventors of the Doctrin of Spirits among the Heathens, the Egyptian Priests, the Chaldæan Magi, or the Indian Bramins. PAUSANIAS is very positive in favour of the two last: [2] *For*, says he, *I know the Chaldean and Indian Magi to be the first who affirm'd that the Soul of Man was immortal; and of this they persuaded as well other Greeks, as especially* PLATO *the Son of* ARISTON. A few more Greeks besides PAUSANIAS (and from their Authority some

---

[1] Theodoret. de Græc. Affect. Serm. 2. Theodor. Melitenior. Proœm. in Astronomiam. Amm. Marcell. l. 22.

[2] Εγω δε Χαλδαιους και Ινδων τους Μαγους πρωτους οιδα ειποντας, ως αθανατος εστιν ανθρωπου ψυχη: και σφισι και Ελληνων αλλοι τε επεισθησαν, και ουχ ηκιστα Πλατων ὁ Αριστωνος. Messeniac.

of

of the Roman Writers) believ'd the Chaldæans to have bin at least the Inventors of Astrology, if not of the Soul's Immortality. But we might produce an Army of Witnesses, if the things did not speak themselves, to prove that the Chaldæans (to whom the Bramins[1] were Disciples) had all their Learning and Religion, and consequently the Immortality of the Soul, no less than Astrology, from the Egyptians. We cou'd show that MACROBIUS[2] did not exaggerate, when he call'd Egypt *the Mother of the Sciences*, and its Inhabitants *the Parents of all the Arts in Philosophy, the first of all Men that dar'd to search and measure the Heavens*, and *the only Persons skill'd in all Divine things*; that is to say, the best Divines then in the World. But such a Disquisition not being absolutely ne-

Letter II.

[1] Κλεαρχος δε ὁ Σολευς, εν τῳ περι παιδειας, και τους Γυμνοσοφιστας απογονους ειναι των Μαγων φησιν. Diog. Laert. in Proæmio Histor. Philosophorum.

[2] Dies quidem hic intercalaris, antequam quintus Annus incipiat inserendus, cum Ægypti matris Artium ratione consentit. *Saturnal. lib.* 1. *c.* 15. Plato Ægyptios omnium Philosophiæ Disciplinarum Parentes secutus est. *Somn. Scip. l.* 1. *c.* 19. Quos constat primos omnium Cœlum scrutari & metiri ausos. *Ibid. c.* 21. Imitatus Ægyptios solos divinarum rerum omnium conscios. *Saturnal. l.* 1. *c.* 14.

Letter II. cessary here, we must be content with just what makes for our purpose.

8. THOSE who attributed the Invention of Religion to the Chaldæans, had no reason but their becoming so famous for Astrology (which they first taught the Greeks) and the mighty Noise which they made every where about Spirits and Dæmons, their Hierarchy of Angels, the final Conflagration of the World, and several other Notions like to these. But this Assertion is easily overthrown by more antient and numerous Authoritys. HERODOTUS, the Father of History, says that [*] *the Egyptians were the first of Men who instituted Assemblys, Shows, and Pilgrimages in honour of the Gods*, and *that from them the Greeks have learnt it; of which* he alledges *for a Proof, that these Things were practis'd from remote Times by the Egyptians, whereas but very lately by the Greeks.* 'Tis confest by all that

---

[*] Πανηγυριας δε αρα και πομπας και προσαγωγας πρωτοι ανθρωπων Αιγυπτιοι εισι οι ποιησαμενοι; και παρα τουτων οι Ἑλληνες μεμαθηκασι. Τεκμηριον δε μοι τουτου τοδε. Ἁι μεν γαρ φαινονται εκ πολλου τευ χρονου ποιευμεναι, ἁι δε Ἑλληνικαι νεωστι εποιηθησαν. L. 2.

the

the Athenians had a great part of their Worship from their King CECROPS an Egyptian; they had many Customs from DANAUS and his Daughters of the same Country, and the Eleusinian and Samothracian Mysterys were only Copys from those of ISIS and OSIRIS. As to Astrology particularly, HERODOTUS maintains, [1] That *the Egyptians first invented what Month and Day shou'd belong to each God, and on whatever Day any Person was to be born, what was to be his Lot, what Death he shou'd die, and how he shou'd live; and that these things were made use of by such Greeks as were addicted to Poetry.* To the same purpose DION CASSIUS says, [2] That *the Disposition of the Days according to the seven Planets was the Invention of the Egyptians, tho not communicated to all other People but very lately; and that it was utterly unknown to*

Letter II.

[1] Και ταδε αλλα Αιγυπτιοισι εστι εξευρημενα: μεις τε και ἡμερη ἑκαστη θεων ὁτευ εστι; και τῃ εκαστῃ ἡμερῃ γενομενος ὁτεοισι εγκυρησει; και ὁκως τελευτησει, και ὁκοιος τις εσται. Και τουτοισι των Ἑλληνων οἱ εν ποιησει γενομενοι εχρησαντο. Lib. 2.

[2] Το δε δη ες τους αστερας τους επτα τους πλανητας ωνομασμενους τας ἡμερας ανακεισθαι, κατεστη μεν ὑπ' Αιγυπτιων, παρεστι δε και επι παντας ανθρωπους ου παλαι ποτε, ὡς λογῳ ειπειν, αρξαμενον. Οἱ γουν αρχαιοι Ἑλληνες ουδαμῃ αυτο, ὁσα γε εμε ειδεναι ηπισταντο. Lib. 37.

Letter II.

the old Grecians. HERODOTUS again acquaints us with what the Egyptians affirm'd from their own most antient Records,[1] That *they had first in use the Sirnames of the twelve greater Gods, and that the Greeks borrow'd these things of them: that they were likewise the first who appointed Altars, and Statues, and Shrines for the Gods, and to carve Animals in Stone.* This is further confirm'd by LUCIAN, whose Words are these: [2] *The Egyptians are said to be the first of Men who had the Knowleig of the Gods, who built Temples, and instituted Shrines and Assemblys. They were likewise the first who understood the sacred Names* or Words, *and the first that taught the sacred Discourses* or Language. *But not long after the Assyrians learnt the Doctrin of the Gods from the Egyptians; they*

---

[1] Δυωδεκα τε θεων επωνυμιας ελεγον πρωτους Αιγυπτιους νομισαι, και Ελληνας παρα σφεων αναλαβειν· βωμους τε και αγαλματα και νηους θεοισι απονειμαι σφεας πρωτους, και ζωα εν λιθοισι εγγλυψαι. Lib. 2.

[2] Πρωτοι μεν ανθρωπων Αιγυπτιοι λεγονται θεων τε εννοιην λαβειν, και ιρα εισασθαι, και τεμενεα και πανηγυριας αποδεξαι. Πρωτοι δε και ουνοματα ιρα εγνωσαν, και λογους ιρους ελεξαν. Μετα δε ου πολλω χρονω παρ' Αιγυπτιων λογον Ασσυριοι ες θεους ηκουσαν, και ιρα και νηους ηγειραν, εν τοισι και αγαλματα εθεντο, και ξοανα εστησαντο. Το δε παλαιον και παρ' Αιγυπτιοισι αξοανοι νηοι εσαν. De Dea Syria.

Letter II.

also built Temples and Shrines, and in these they plac'd Images and erected Statues: yet of old the Temples of the Egyptians were without any Statues. Here are decisive Passages against the Assyrians and the Greeks. But let's hear [1] DIODORUS SICULUS of the Magi in particular. *The Egyptians,* says he, *affirm that many Colonys were spread over the World out of their Country. For* BELUS, *who is reckon'd the Son of* NEPTUNE *and* LIBYA, *led a Colony into the Land of Babylon; and having fixt his Seat near the River Euphrates, he did after the manner of the Egyptians institute Priests, exempting them from publick and expensive Offices; and by the Babylonians they are stil'd Chaldeans, who observe the Stars after the Example of the Priests, and natural Philosophers, and Astrologers of Egypt.* This is back'd

[1] Οἱ δὲ ἐν Αἰγύπτιοι φασι και μετα ταυτα αποικιας πλειστας εξ Αιγυπτε κατα πασαν διασπαρηναι την οικεμενην: εις Βαβυλωνα μεν γαρ αγαγειν αποικες Βηλον τον νομιζομενον Ποσειδωνος ειναι και Λιβυης: ὃν παρα τον Ευφρατην ποταμον καθιδρυνθεντα, τες δε ιερεις καθαστησασθαι παραπλησιως τοις κατ' Αιγυπτον ατελεις, και πασης λειτεργιας απολελυμενες, ες Βαβυλωνιοι καλεσι Χαλδαιες: τας τε παρατηρησεις των αστρων ποιεισθαι, μιμεμενες της παρ' Αιγυπτιοις ιερεις, και φυσικες, ετι δε αστρολογες. Lib. 1.

Letter II. by [1] PAUSANIAS, who says, That BELUS *the Babylonian had his Name from* BELUS *an Egyptian the Son of* LIBYA. And [2] DIODORUS repeats once again, That *the Egyptians said the Chaldeans of Babylon were descended from them, and that they learnt from the Egyptian Priests that Astrology which gave them so much Reputation.* To tire you with no more Proofs, the Egyptians had many opportunitys to spread their Doctrins in Asia as well as in Africa (especially before the Assyrian Monarchy) by the prodigious Conquests of SESOSTRIS and his Successors even into India, much further than ALEXANDER the Great cou'd penetrate many Ages afterwards. SESOSTRIS was likewise in Thracia, and some other Parts of Europe. [3] NECEPSOS, another Egyptian King, is related to have taught many mysterious Rites to the Magi, the Sciences not being then un-

---

[1] 'Ο εν Βαβυλωνι Βηλος απο ανδρος Αιγυπτιυ Βηλυ τυ Λιβυης ονομα εχει. Messeniac.

[2] Φασι δε τυς εν Βαβυλωνι Χαλδαιυς αποικυς Αιγυπτιων οντας, την Δοξαν εχειν την περι της Αστρολογιας παρα των Ἱερεων μαθοντας των Αιγυπτιων. Lib. I.

[3] Quique Magos docuit Mysteria vana Necepsos.
Auson. Epist. 19.

worthy

worthy of Princes; for [1] PORPHYRY tells us, That *the Race of the Magi was so potent and honorable among the Persians, that* DARIUS *the Son of* HYSTASPES *caus'd to be* [2] *inscrib'd among other things, on his own Monument, that he was Master to the Magi.* I know the Jews and a world of Christians pretend that the Egyptians had all their Learning from ABRAHAM, a Chaldean by Nation, tho not by Profession, a Stranger who liv'd there only two years, and who probably spoke a different Language. The Pentateuch makes no mention of his Learning; or if he understood Astronomy or any other Science, why did he not take the same pains to instruct his own Nation as he did the Egyptians? for the Jews were of all Eastern People the most illiterate; whereas it is recorded in the Acts of the Apostles for the Honor of MOSES, not that he follow'd the Doctrins of ABRAHAM, but that he was educated and had excell'd in all the Learning of the Egyptians. The C.7. v. 22.

Letter II.

[2] Οὕτω δε μεγα και σεβασμιον γενος τῦτο παρα Περσαις νενομισαι, ὥστε και Δαρειον τον Ὑστάσπε ἐπιγραψαι τῳ μνηματι, προς τοις αλλοις, ὅτι και Μαγικων γεγονε διδασκαλος. De Abstin. Animal. l. 4.

Letter II. Pentateuch it self makes mention of their Religion and Sciences long before the Law was deliver'd to Moses, which is an indisputable Testimony of their Antiquity before any Nation in the World.

9. HAVING thus done Justice to the Egyptians, and proving them to have bin the Fountains of Learning to all the East, the Authors of the Chaldæan and Greek Religions; I come now, SERENA, to show that they were the first among the Heathens, who particularly asserted the Immortality of the Soul, with all that depends on it, as Heaven, Hell, and the intermediate Spaces, Specters, Visions, Sorcery, Necromancy, and all kinds of Divination. Herodotus, who liv'd long in their Country, who convers'd familiarly with their Priests, [a] who carefully distinguishes what he saw, and ask'd, and examin'd, from Hearsay and Report, and who had opportunitys to search into their Antiquity and Opinions the best

---

[a] Μεχει μεν τυτυ οψις δε ἐμοὶ, και γνωμη, και ἱστοριη ταυτα λεγυσα εστι: τοδε απο τυδε, Αιγυπτιυς ερχομαι λογυς ερεων κατα ηκυον, προσεσται δε τι και αυτοισι τι και της εμης οψιος. L. 2.

of

of any body, is very clear and poſitive. Letter II.
[1] *The Egyptians,* ſays he, *were the firſt who maintain'd this Opinion, that* THE SOUL OF MAN IS IMMORTAL; *that the Body being dead, it removes into ſome other Animal that is born; and that when it has taken its Circuit thro all terreſtrial, marine, and volatile Bodys, it enters again into the Body of ſome Man that is born. Now this Courſe is perform'd in the ſpace of three thouſand Years. Certain Greeks have made uſe of this Doctrin, as if it were of their own Invention, ſome ſooner and others later; whoſe Names, tho known to me, I purpoſely forbear to write.* DIODORUS SICULUS acquaints us who [2] they were: and here, to name no other, we ſee whence PYTHAGORAS had his Tranſmigration, of which I ſhall have

[1] Πρωτοι δε και τονδε τον λογον Αιγυπτιοι εισι ειποντες, ὡς ανθρωπου ψυχη αθανατος εστι; του σωματος δε καταφθινοντος, ες αλλο ζωον αιει γινομενον εσδυεται; επεαν δε περιελθῃ παντα τα χερσαια, και τα θαλασσια, και τα πετεινα, αυτις ες ανθρωπου σωμα γινομενον εσδυνειν. Την περιηλυσιν δε αυτῃ γινεσθαι εν τρισχιλιοισι ετεσι. Τουτῳ τῳ λογῳ εισι οἱ Ἑλληνων εχρησαντο, οἱ μεν προτερον, οἱ δε ὑστερον, ὡς ιδιῳ εαυτων εοντι, των εγω ειδως τα ουνοματα ου γραφω. L. 2.

[2] Orpheus, Muſæus, Melampus, Dædalus, Homerus, Lycurgus, Solon, Plato, Pythagoras, Eudoxus, Democritus, Œnopis. l. 1. Alii alios nominant.

Letter II. occasion to make some mention before I have done. Thus it was with other Doctrins. Yet, as I hinted before, because the Greeks learnt most of their Astronomy and Astrology from the Magi, they imagin'd them to have invented those Sciences: for by reason of their Colonys in Asia and in the Ionian Islands, they were acquainted with the Magi, much sooner than with the Egyptian Prophets, having little knowledg of the latter, till Egypt was conquer'd by the Persians, and till the time of ALEXANDER the Great; travelling afterwards very frequently thither, and in great numbers.

10. THE Getes learnt the Immortality of the Soul from their Countryman ZAMOLXIS, who was Servant and Disciple to PYTHAGORAS, and who so wrought by his [1] Address on those Scythian Nations, that they not only receiv'd Laws from him, and the Doctrin of a future State; but so great was their Respect towards him

[1] Herodot. l. 4. Strabo l. 16. Mnaseas & Hellanicus in Etymologico magno. Porphyr. in vita Pythag. Diog. Laert. in Pythagora.

for

for these Benefits, that after his Death they worship'd him as a God. This Opinion of changing the present Life for a better, made them so fearless in Battel, and so ready to [1] expose themselves to the greatest Dangers, being continually fir'd to a noble Emulation by their Poets, who (like the [2] Gallick Bards) eterniz'd the Memory of those magnanimous Worthys that lost their Lives in War. The Druids of Gaule (of whom were issu'd those in Britain) who were of the same Persuasion with the Getes, and who taught the Transmigration of Souls, borrow'd their Letters from the Greeks, and probably their Philosophy, as JULIUS CÆSAR in [3] express words informs us. This might easily be done by means of the most antient Greek Colony of Marseilles, famous for Arts and Learning. They might have a Communication with those of the Grecian Country and Religion behind them in Italy. And from their Neighbors the Germans

[1] Pompon. Mela l. 2. c. 2. cum aliis pæne innumeris.

[2] Cæsar de Bello Gal. l. 6. Pompon. Mela l. 3. c. 2. Amm. Marcel. l. 15. Plinius aliique.

[3] Cum in reliquis fere Rebus, publicis privatisque Rationibus, Græcis Litteris utantur. Lib. 6. de Bello Gallico.

(who

Letter II. (who are often comprehended under the the name of Celts as well as themselves) they might likewise receive the Doctrin of ZAMOLXIS. But however this cou'd happen, LUCAN in the first Book of his *Pharsalia*, sings of all those Nations in this manner.

The numerous Peoples of the frozen North
Are truly happy in their fond Mistake,
Not fearing Death that dreadfullest of Fears.
Hence their rough Minds are always bent on Arms,
Hence their stout Heroes smiling meet their Death,
And hence they think it Cowardise to spare
A Life, that's certain to return again.

11. BUT tho I have trac'd this Opinion to its Source, yet your Question, MADAM, is still unresolv'd, till I

* ——— Certe populi, quos despicit Arctos,
Felices errore suo, quos, ille Timorum,
Maximus, haud urget Lethi metus. Inde ruendi
In Ferrum mens prona viris, Animæque capaces
Mortis, & ignavum rediturae parcere vitæ.

explain

explain how the Egyptians themselves could frame such a Notion without Divine Revelation. To this I answer, that their Funeral Rites, and their historical Method of preserving the Memory of deserving Persons, seem in all probability to have bin the occasional Causes of this Belief. Their way of burying, you know, was by embalming the dead Bodys, which they deposited in subterranean Grots, where they continu'd intire for thousands of Years; so that before any Notion of separate or immortal Souls, the common Language was, that such a one was under ground, that he was carry'd over the River Acherusia by CHARON (the Title of the publick Ferryman for this purpose) and laid happily to rest in the Elysian Fields, which were the common Burial-place near Memphis. Among other Methods they had of perpetuating Events, the surest of all was to impose the Names of memorable Persons and Things on the Constellations, as the only eternal Monuments, nor subject to the Violence of Men or Brutes, nor to the Injury of Time or Weather. This Custom was deriv'd from them to other Nations, who chang'd indeed the Names, but gave new ones to the Stars for

Letter II.

Letter II. [illegible] and the [illegible] and [illegible] and [illegible] Mo[illegible] were [illegible] ground. [illegible] hearing [illegible] [illegible] Ci[illegible] Dead [illegible] on the [illegible] which [illegible] so [illegible] the Flames and Torments of Hell.

[illegible] ABOUT the Life of those in the Stars I shall speak more largely here-after [illegible], when I have leisure to write the Discourse I promis'd you about the Origin of Idolatry. But at present I shall proceed with their Funeral Rites, which were the occasion of so many

---

[1] In Terram [illegible] Corporibus, [illegible] humo tectis, sub Terra censebant reliquam vitam agi Mortuorum. *Tusc. Quæst. l.* 1.

Opinions

Opinions relating to a future State in Egypt, in other Parts of Africa, over all Asia, in many places of Europe, and particularly in Greece. DIODORUS SICULUS, in the first Book of his unvaluable *Library*, very largely relates the Funeral Rites of the Egyptians, especially their manner of embalming Bodys to such Perfection, that after many Ages the same Likeness and Lineaments continue: after which he proceeds in these words. [a] *The Relations of the Body that is to be bury'd, acquaint before-hand the Judges, and the Kindred as well as the Friends of the dead Person with the Day of his Burial: and after telling his Name, they certify that he is at that time to pass over the Lake. After this there assemble above forty Judges, and sitting in a certain Semicircle, prepar'd on the side of the Lake, the Boat, which is provided in the mean while*

Letter II.

---

[a] Του δε μελλοντος θαπτεσθαι σωματος ὁι συγγενεις προλεγουσι την ἡμεραν της ταφης τοις δε δικασταις και τοις συγγενεσιν, ετι δε φιλοις του τετελευτηκοτος; και διαβεβαιουνται, λεγοντες ὅτι διαβαινειν μελλει την λιμνην τοὔνομα του τετελευτηκοτος. Επειτα παραγενομενων δικαστων πλειονων των τετταρακοντα, και καθιζοντων επι τινος ἡμικυκλιου, κατεσκευασμενου περαν της λιμνης; ἡ μεν βαρις καθελκεται κατεσκευασμενη προτερον ὑπο των ταυτην

Letter II.

while by those to whom that Care belongs, is brought thither by the Ferryman, whom the Egyptians in their Language call CHARON. *Wherefore they say that* ORPHEUS, *having seen this Custom when he had formerly travel'd into Egypt, compos'd his Fable about Hell, partly imitating these things, and partly inventing out of his own Head.* Then DIODORUS goes on to tell that every body may accuse or defend the dead Person, who, if he be prov'd to have led a bad Life, is deny'd the usual sort of Burial. From this Prohibition of Burial in Egypt, which was afflicting to the Living and scandalous to the Dead, the Greeks (and from them the Romans) had their Notion that the Souls of the unbury'd were disquieted, and cou'd not pass over the River into the Elysian Fields, turning a noble Practice into a senseless Fable. Hence you may likewise perceive how they came by the Notion of infernal Judges, which Office

---

ταυτην εχοντων την επιμελειαν; εφεστηκε δε ταυτη πορθμευς, ὃν Αιγυπτιοι κατα την ιδιαν Διαλεκτον ονομαζουσι Χαρωνα. Διο και φασιν Ορφεα το παλαιον εις Αιγυπτον παραβαλοντα και θεασαμενον τετο το νομιμον, μυθοποιησαι τα καθ' ᾁδε; τα μεν μιμησαμενον, τα δ' αυτον ιδια πλασαμενον.

they

they bestow'd on MINOS, ÆACUS, and RHADAMANTHUS, the most just Princes among the Greeks. But not to digress, if any false Accuser appear'd, he was severely punish'd; and if none accus'd the dead, then he was put into his Coffin, and his Relations throwing off their Mourning, made a solemn Panegyrick, not magnifying his Dignity or Family, but commending his Education, Piety, Justice, Temperance, and other Virtues. After relating more Particularitys to our purpose, DIODORUS makes this most judicious Observation. [1] *The Greeks,* says he, *in their commentitious Fables, and by their celebrated Poets have disguiz'd the Truth of these things, as of what relates to the Honor of the Just and Disgrace of the Wicked; and therefore they have bin so far from being able by these means to lead Men to the best sort of Life, that they are themselves despis'd by the Bad, and derided for their Folly. But among the*

Letter II.

E

[1] Ὁ μεν γαρ Ἑλληνες μυθοις πεπλασμενοις και ποιηταις διαβεβλημενοις την αει τελων πιστιν παραδεδωκασι, την τε των ευσεβων τιμην, και την των πονηρων τιμωριαν. Τοιγαρουν ουχ' οιως ισχυουσι δυνασθαι ταυτα προτρεψασθαι επι τον αριστον βιον τους ανθρωπους; αλλα τουναντιον υπο των φαυλων χλευαζομενοι, καταφρονησεως τυγχανουσι.

Παρ

Letter II. *the Egyptians, the Punishment of the Wicked and the Recompence of the Good, not being contain'd in Fables, but exhibited to our Eyes, each Party is every day put in mind of their Dutys; and by this Custom there grows the best and most useful Reformation of Manners.* Lower in the same Book he gives a Catalogue of such celebrated Greek Philosophers and Legislators as were initiated in the Egyptian Learning; and repeats again, that ORPHEUS [1] *brought from thence the greatest part of the mysterious Rites* (us'd in Greece) *with the Orgys that are celebrated at their Explanation, and the Fictions of Hell.* Somewhat lower again, he, that was an Eye-witness, assures us, That [2] *the Meadow, which was the feign'd Habitation of the Dead, is a place by the Lake call'd Acherusia near Memphis,*

Παρα δε τοις Αιγυπτιοις ου μυθωδους αλλ' ορατης τοις μεν πονηροις της κολασεως, τοις δ' αγαθοις της τιμης ουσης, καθ' εκαστην ημεραν αμφοτεροι των εαυτοις προσηκοντων υπομιμνησκονται; και δια τουτου τε τροπου μεγιστη και συμφορωτατη διορθωσις γινεται των ηθων. Lib. I.

[1] Ορφεα μεν γαρ των μυστικων τελετων τα πλειστα, και τα περι την εαυτου πλανην οργιαζομενα, και την των εν αδου μυθολογιαν απενεγκασθαι. Ibid.

[2] Λειμωνα δε νομιζειν και την μυθολογουμενην οικησιν των μετηλλαχοτων τον παρα την λιμνην τοπον την καλουμενην

phis, which City is surrounded with most beautiful Meads and Groves of Lotus and Calamus. Nor is it improperly said that the Dead inhabit those places; for that the greatest part and the most sumptuous of the Egyptian Burials are made here, the dead Bodys being transported over the River and Acherusian Lake, and laid there in Grots made for that purpose. The other Fictions of the Greeks about Hell, do likewise agree with those things which are to this day perform'd in Egypt: for the Vessel for transporting the Bodys is call'd Baris, and a piece of Mony to the value of an Obolus is paid for fraught to the Ferryman, who in their Country Language is call'd CHARON. *There is also near those places, as they say, the Fane of* Letter II.

E 2 *darksom*

μενην μεν Αχερουσιαν, πλησιον δε ουσαν της Μεμφεως, οντων περι αυτην λειμωνων καλλιστων, ἑλων, και λωτου και καλαμου. Ακολουθως δ' ειρησθαι και το κατοικειν τους τελευτησαντας εν τουτοις τοις τοποις: δια το τας των Αιγυπτιων τας πλειστας και μεγιστας ενταυθα γινεσθαι, διαπορθμευομενων μεν των νεκρων δια τε του ποταμου και της Αχερουσιας λιμνης, τιθεμενων δε των σωματων εις τας ενταυθα κειμενας θηκας. Συμφωνειν δε και τ' αλλα τα παρα τοις Ἑλλησι καθ' ᾅδου μυθολογουμενα τοις ετι νυν γινομενοις κατ' Αιγυπτον: το μεν γαρ διακομιζον τα σωματα πλοιον, Βαριν καλεισθαι; το δ' επιβαθρον νομισμα τον οβολον τῳ πορθμει διδοσθαι, καλουμενῳ κατα την εγχωριον διαλεκτον Χαρωνι. Ειναι δε λεγουσι πλησιον των τοπων τουτων και σκοτιας Ἑκατης ἱερον, και πυλας Κωκυτου

Letter II. *darksom* HECATE, *and the Gates of* COCYTUS *and* LETHE *made fast with brazen Bolts. There are also other Portals of Truth, and near these the Statue of Justice without a Head. There yet remain among the Egyptians several other things that gave occasion to our Fables, keeping still the same Names, and the same Actions being perform'd.* Here's a most natural Account of the Rise of those Poetical Fictions concerning the Elysian Fields, CHARON and his Passage-mony, with the different Mansions of departed Souls, and the several Portals of Hell. All other Origins are false, or manifestly absurd and precarious. This whole Book of the most accurate DIODORUS deserves to be read: but I have transcrib'd enough for my purpose.

13. THUS have I shown you, MADAM, how this Opinion of the Souls Immortality, and the Consequences

---

κυ]ῶ και Ληθης, διειλημμενας χαλκεοις οχευσιν: ὑπαρχειν δε και αλλας πυλας Αληθειας, και πλησιον τουτων ειδωλον ακεφαλον ἑσταναι Δικης: πολλα δε και αλλα των μεμυθολογημενων διαμενειν παρ' Αιγυπτιοις, τηρουμενης ἐτι της προσηγοριας και της εν τω πραττειν ενεργειας. Ibid.

of the ſame, was introduc'd from the Egyptians among the Grecians, ſpread by the latter in their Colonys in Aſia and Europe, and deliver'd to the Romans, who from the Greeks had their Religion and Laws. I mark'd the Progreſs of it among the Scythians, Germans, Gauls, and Britains. I have likewiſe prov'd how from Egypt, the Place of its Birth, it travel'd to the Chaldæans and Indians, and from them over all the Eaſtern Parts of the World: for 'tis no wonder that this Doctrin was gladly and univerſally receiv'd (tho not built among the Heathens on its true Reaſons) ſince it flatter'd Men with the Hopes of what they wiſh above all things whatſoever, namely, to continue their Exiſtence beyond the Grave; there being but few that can bear the very Thoughts of ever ceaſing to live ſomewhere, and moſt People commonly chuſing to be miſerable, rather than not to be at all. This was the State of the Soul's Immortality, among thoſe Nations who were not illuminated by Divine Revelation. The People begun it, from them their Children learnt it, at laſt it became a part of all mens Education (as it happens to Opinions generally receiv'd) and ſo the Learned

Letter II. themselves believ'd it before they had a reason for it. 'Tis true, the Vulgar, who are not us'd to Reflections, embrac'd it ever afterwards (as they do still) upon Trust or from Authority: but not so with the Philosophers, who offer'd many probable Arguments for the Soul's separate Existence and eternal Duration. They conceiv'd their own Thoughts or Ideas to be immaterial, and to have nothing in common with Extension; they found a Freedom in their Wills, and a spontaneous Motion in their Bodys; they observ'd a perpetual Contention between their Appetite and their Reason; they laid much stress on their Dreams, and thought that sometimes awake they had certain Presages in their Minds of future Dangers; they saw that Men had an unquenchable Thirst after Knowledg, a Prospect of Futurity, and earnestly desir'd a Happiness that shou'd never end: therefore they concluded that all these things must needs proceed from some Being distinct from the Body, which was self-moving, and consequently immortal; since every Parcel of Matter is mov'd by some external Cause, and that what has Motion in it self can never lose it. The Soul's Immortality was likewise greatly ly confirm'd among the Heathens by their Legislators, whereof several did not believe it themselves; but (observing that tho some were vertuous by Nature or Temper, and that others were made so by the hopes of Reward and Honor, or by the Fear of Punishment and Disgrace) they further adopted this Opinion, as suting all mens Circumstances, persuading them that in the other Life, the Wicked were sure to be punish'd for their Crimes, tho they might here escape the Rigor of the Laws; and that the Good wou'd likewise meet there with those Rewards, which might be unjustly deny'd to their Merit in the present Life. By others this Argument was deem'd to have more of Reason than of Politicks in it, and they have labor'd to prove that such a Conduct was necessarily becoming the Goodness and Equity of a most wise Being. They had several Disputes about the Soul's Præ-existence, Duration, Essence, and the Manner and Time of its coming into the Body, its leaving of it, and their Union together. On these Subjects there have bin written many subtil and ingenious Conjectures, but more that were ridiculous, extravagant, and impossible. Nor have the Letter II.

Letter II. modern Philosophers succeeded any better than the Antients, and among both of them scarce any two were of a mind; whereas in my opinion the Moderns have not the same right to examine this matter as the Antients, but ought humbly to acquiesce in the Authority of our Savior JESUS CHRIST, who brought Life and Immortality to Light.

14. 'TIS no wonder that a Notion, thus grounded among the Heathens, was doubted or deny'd by great numbers of them, even by whole Sects, as the Epicureans for example; and in some other Sects the distinct Being of it after Death was totally destroy'd, they making it then to return to the Soul of the World, and to be swallow'd up therein. But in all Sects there never wanted particular Persons who really oppos'd the Soul's Immortality, tho they might accommodate their ordinary Language to the Belief of the People: for most of the Philosophers (as we read) had two sorts of Doctrins, the one internal and the other external, or the one private and the other publick; the latter to be indifferently communicated to all the World, and the former only very cautiously to their best Friends,

or to ſome few others capable of receiving it, and that wou'd not make any ill uſe of the ſame. PYTHAGORAS himſelf did not believe the Tranſmigration which has made him ſo famous to Poſterity; for in the internal or ſecret Doctrin he meant no more than the eternal Revolution of Forms in Matter, thoſe ceaſleſs Viciſſitudes and Alterations, which turn every thing into all things, and all things into any thing, as Vegetables and Animals become part of us, we become part of them, and both become parts of a thouſand other things in the Univerſe, Earth turning into Water, Water into Air, Air into Æther, and ſo back again in Mixtures without End or Number. But in the external or popular Doctrin he impos'd on the Mob by an equivocal Expreſſion, that *they ſhou'd become various kinds of Beaſts after Death*, thereby to deter 'em the more effectually from Wickedneſs. Take notice, MADAM, how his intimate Acquaintance and Diſciple TIMÆUS LOCRUS ſpeaks. [1] *If any Perſon*, ſays he, *will continue impenitent and refractory, he ſhall be ſure of Puniſhment both from the Laws, and*

from

[1] Εἰ δὲ κά τις σκληρὸς καὶ ἀπειθὴς, τήνῳ δ' ἑπέσθω κόλασις, ἅ τ' ἐκ τῶν νόμων καὶ ἁ ἐκ τῶν λόγων συν-

τονα

Letter II.

from those Doctrins, which denounce celestial and infernal Judgments; as that unhappy Ghosts will meet with implacable Torments, and those other things which the Ionick Poet has deliver'd out of antient Tradition. For as we cure the Bodys of sick Persons with any sort of Remedys, if they refuse the most wholesom; so we keep the Minds of Men in order by false Reasons, if they will not be govern'd by true ones. Wherefore there is a necessity of teaching those foreign Torments: as that there is a Transmigration of the Soul, those of Cowards passing into female Bodys assign'd 'em for a Disgrace; those of Murderers into Beasts of Prey, for a Punishment; those of luxurious Persons, into the Forms of Swine or Goats; those of inconstant and boasting Fellows, into Animals flying in the Air; and those of the Slothful and the

---

τοια επαγοισα δειματα τε επουρανια και τα καθ' ἅδεω; ὅτι κολασιες απαραιτητοι αποκειν]αι δυσδαιμοσι νερτεροις, και τ'αλλα ὅσα επαινεω τον Ιονικον ποιηταν, εκ παλαιας ποιευντα τως εναγεας. Ὡς γαρ τα σωματα νοσωδεσι ποκα ὑγιασομες, εικα μη εικῃ τοις ὑγιεινοτατοις; ὕτω τας ψυχας απειργομες ψευδεσι λογοις, εικα μη αγηται αλαθεσι. Λεγοιντο δ'αναγκαιως και τιμωριαι ξεναι, ὡς μετενδυομεναν ταν ψυχαν, των μεν δειλων ες γυναικεα σκανεα, ποθ' ὕβριν εκδιδομενα; των δε μιαιφονων ες θηριων σωματα, ποτι κολασιν; λαγνων δ'ες συων η καπρων μορφας; κουφων δε και μετεωρων

the Idle, of the Unteachable and the Foolish, into the Shapes of Animals living in the Water. HOMER's Tradition of the Torments of Hell I have prov'd already to have bin from Egypt; and Transmigration is here call'd a foreign Torment, because PYTHAGORAS learnt it of the Egyptian Priests. Letter II.

15. THO the Poets embellish'd their Pieces with the Opinion of the Soul's Immortality, yet a great number of them (for they were not all of a mind) utterly rejected it, as I might show by their own express words: for SENECA [1] was not single in saying,

> *Nought's after Death, and Death it*
> *self is nought,*
> *Of a quick Race only the utmost Goal;*
> *Then may the Saints lose all their*
> *Hopes of Heav'n,*
> *And Sinners quit their racking Fears*
> *of Hell.*

But

μετεωρων εις πτηνων αμαρτορων; αργων δε και απαιδευτων, αμαθων τε και ανοητων, εις την των ενυδρων ιδεαν. In Libri Calce.

[1] Post Mortem nihil est, ipsaque Mors nihil,
Velocis spatii Meta novissima.
Spem ponant avidi, solliciti Metum.

Quæris

Letter II.

But after Death you're curious where
to be?
E'en where the Children yet unborn
remain.
We're lost in Darkness and devouring
Time.
Death wasts the Body, and at last de-
stroys;
Nor spares the Soul. Infernal Depths,
and those
Dark Kingdoms of th' inexorable
Lord,
With Cerb'rus guarding the well-bolted
Gates,
Are only senseless Tales and empty
Words,
A Fable like unto a frightful Dream.

The best reason I can find for the Incredulity of the Poets, is the Experience they had of their own Fictions about the future State of the Soul: for scarce

---

Quæris quo jaceas post obitum loco?
Quo non nata jacent.
Tempus nos avidum devorat & Chaos.
Mors individua est noxia Corpori,
Nec parcens Animæ. Tænara, & aspero
Regnum sub Domino, Limen & obsidens
Custos non facili Cerberus ostio,
Rumores vacui, verbaque inania,
Et par sollicito Fabula Somnio.
Troad. Act. 2. Chor.

one

one of 'em believ'd the charming Descriptions they made of the Elysian Fields, nor their terrible tho elegant Relations of the Torments of the Wicked. VIRGIL, the most accurate and ample Topographer of the infernal Regions, cou'd yet, when he thought of EPICURUS, break out into this Philosophical Rapture: Letter II.

[1] *Happy! who cou'd of things the Causes know,*
Cur'd of all Fears, who cou'd tread under foot
Relentless Fate, and greedy Waves of Hell!

I shou'd never have done if I alledg'd all the Passages where HORACE, JUVENAL, and the rest of them sport with the storys about Hell, and Ghosts, and the like: but CORNELIUS SEVERUS has exprest the Minds of them all, tho after a more serious manner, in his Poem concerning the burning of Mount Etna.

---

[1] Felix qui potuit rerum cognoscere Causas,
Atque Metus omnes & inexorabile Fatum
Subjecit pedibus, strepitumque Acherontis avari!
Georg. l. 2.

Of

Letter II.

[1] *Of all our Errors and Mistakes of things*
The greatest part proceeds from tragick Scenes.
In Verse the Poets, not in Vision, saw
Black airy Spirits fleeting under ground,
And PLUTO'*s pallid Regions after Death.*
The Poets feign'd the Stygian Waves and Dogs.
These have foul TITYUS *o'er sev'n Acres stretch'd;*
'Tis they, poor TANTALUS, *who thee torment*
With Hunger merciless and Thirst; 'tis they,
O MINOS *and* O EACUS, *who sing*
Your splendid Judgments upon trembling Souls;

'Tis

[1] Plurima pars Scenæ rerum est fallacia: Vates
Sub terris nigros viderunt Carmine Manes,
Atque inter cineres Ditis pallentia Regna.
Mentiti vates Stygias Undasque, Canesque.
Hi Tityon septem stravere in jugera fœdum;
Sollicitant magna te circum, Tantale, pœna,
Sollicitantque Siti; Minos, tuaque, Æace, in umbris
Jura

'Tis they who turn IXION's *rest-* Letter II.
less Wheel,
And forge all th' other Fables under
Earth.
Earth's not enough: they pry about
the Gods,
And boldly view that Heaven where they
ne'er shall come.

You'l think me uncharitable, perhaps, for excluding them by this last Line out of Paradise: but, besides that they deserve no less for their Fictions in prejudice of Truth, the Injury's not so great; since they cannot much fear a Hell of their own making.

16. BUT the Reasons of those who deny'd the Immortality of the Soul, whether Poets or Philosophers, are almost all comprehended in a narrow Compass by PLINY the elder, in the seventh Book of his *Natural History*. ¹ *After the Interment of the Body*, says he, *there are various Conjectures about departed*

Jura canunt; idemque rotant Ixionis orbem;
Quicquid & interius falsi sibi conscia Terra est.
Non est Terra satis: speculantur Numina Divum,
Nec metuunt oculos alieno admittere Cœlo, &c.

¹ Post sepulturam variæ Manium Ambages. Omnibus a suprema die eadem quæ ante primam; nec magis

Letter II. *parted Souls. But the State of all Men is the same after the last Day of their Life, as before the first; nor is there any more Sense in Body or Soul after Death, than before the Day of our Birth. Yet the Vanity of living Men extends to future Ages, and feigns to it self a new Life in the very time of Death: some bestowing Immortality on the Soul; some teaching the Transmigration of the same; others allowing Sense to those in Hell, and worshipping their Ghosts, and making a God of him, who is not at present so much as a Man. As if indeed the manner of breathing in Man differ'd any way from that of all other Animals; or as if there cou'd not be found many things which enjoy a longer Life, to which no body dreams of attributing the like Immortality. But what sort of Body has the separate Soul? Of what Substance? Where*

---

magis a morte sensus ullus aut Corpori aut Animæ, quam ante Natalem. Eadem enim Vanitas in futurum etiam se prorogat, & in mortis quoque tempore ipsa sibi vitam mentitur: alias Immortalitatem Animæ; alias Transfigurationem; alias sensum Inferis dando, & Manes colendo, Deumque faciendo qui jam etiam Homo esse desierit. Ceu vero ullo modo spirandi ratio Homini a cæteris Animalibus distet; aut non diuturniora multa in vita reperiantur, quibus nemo similem divinat Immortalitatem. Quod autem Corpus Animæ per

Where resides its Thinking? How does it see? How does it hear? Or by what means does it touch? About what is it busy'd? Or what Good can there be without these things? Where likewise is the Mansion thereof? And in so many Ages, how vast must be the multitude of Souls, as well as of Ghosts! These are Allurements to quiet Children, and the Fictions of Mortals that wou'd live without end. The Vanity of preserving the Bodys of Men, is like that of the Resurrection promis'd by DEMOCRITUS, *who did not revive himself. But what a prodigious Madness is it, to think that Life can be renew'd by Death? Or what Repose can Mortals ever enjoy, if the Soul be alive above, and the Ghost has Sense below? In earnest, this Fondness and Credulity destroys the Usefulness of* Letter II.

F Death,

per se? Quæ Materia? Ubi Cogitatio illi? Quomodo visus? Auditus? Aut qui tangit? Qui usus ejus? Aut quod sine his Bonum? Quæ deinde Sedes? Quantave multitudo tot seculis Animarum, velut Umbrarum! Puerilium ista Deliniméntorum, avidæque nunquam desinere mortalitatis Commenta sunt. Similis & de asservandis Corporibus Hominum, ac reviviscendi promissa Democrito vanitas, qui non revixit ipse. Quæ (malum) ista Dementia est, iterari Vitam morte? Quæve Genitis quies unquam, si in sublimi sensus Animæ manet inter inferos Umbræ? Perdit profecto ista Dulcedo

Letter II. *Death, which is the principal Good of Nature; and doubles the Pains of a dying Man, if he happens to be concern'd about his future State: for if it be a pleasure to live, to whom can it be pleasant to have liv'd? But how much easier and more certain is it for every one to believe his own Experience, and to draw an Argument of his Security from the Consideration of what he has bin before he was born?* Such are the Reasonings of Men who talk all the while of they know not what, having false Notions of the Origin of the Soul, none at all of its Union with the Body, and but imperfect Guesses about its Essence, which leads 'em consequently to doubt of its separate Existence, and so to deny its Immortality. But, however Men left to themselves may mistake, 'tis impossible that God shou'd lie; and what he has reveal'd, tho not in every thing falling under our Comprehension, must yet be true and absolutely certain. And in

---

cedo Credulitasque præcipuum Naturæ bonum, mortem; ac duplicat Obitus, si dolere etiam post-futuri Æstimatione evenit: etenim si dulce vivere est, cui potest esse vixisse? At quanto facilius certiusque sibi quemque credere, ac Specimen securitatis antegenitali sumere experimento? *Cap.* 56.

this

this consists no small Advantage of Believers, that tho they may be equally ignorant with others about the nature of a thing, yet they may have the greatest Conviction of its Existence, and make that use of this Discovery which is benefical or convenient. Letter II.

17. BUT I exceed my design of a bare Historian; besides that you need no Antidote, SERENA, against the Poison of an abler Adversary than PLINY. I have freely given you my Opinion how the Heathens came by their Notion of the Soul's Immortality, with my Reasons for the same: and if I attribute the Invention of this Doctrin, as well as of Astrology, and most of the other Sciences, to the old Egyptians, 'tis not out of any Partiality to an extinct Nation (tho never so learned, wise, or polite) but led by historical Proofs to a full Persuasion. In treading the Mazes of Antiquity, I am secure from all suspicion of Favor or Fear, of Interest or Revenge. I can't be thought to flatter NECEPSOS, if I shou'd make him pass for the King of Astrologers; and I am come too late into the World to expect any Recompence from SESOSTRIS, who, I think, far exceeds all

Letter II. the other Heroes and Conquerors of Antiquity. When I undertook to examine this Subject, the Discovery of Truth was the only end I propos'd to my self, besides that of obeying your Commands, which shall be always, MADAM, receiv'd with more Alacrity and Submission, than those of any Monarch in the Universe, by your most oblig'd and devoted Servant.

LETTER

LETTER III.

The Origin of Idolatry, and Reasons of Heathenism.

1. I AM under a double Obligation, MADAM, to impart my Thoughts to you about *the Origin of Idolatry*, both from the Promise I made you by word of mouth, and by what I have since written to you in the Letter concerning *the Soul's Immortality among the Heathens*. But you are not to expect an account of all the antient Superstitions, which wou'd require many Volumes, nor of any one Religion whatsoever. I shall only endeavour to show by what means the Reason of men became so deprav'd, as to think of subordinate Deitys, how the Worship of many Gods was first

Letter III.

introduc'd into the world, and what induc'd Men to pay Divine Honors to their Fellow-Creatures, whether on Earth or in the Heavens: then I shall explain the Fables of the Heathens by general and certain Principles, giving the occasion of their Temples, Priests, and Altars; of their Images and Statues; their Oracles, Sacrifices, Feasts, Expiations, Judiciary Astrology, Ghosts, and Specters; of the tutelary Powers of several Countrys; of Peoples thinking that Heaven is over us, that Hell is under us, and such other things as commonly occur in the Greek and Roman Authors. Tho with very small pains I could manifestly prove that in Egypt [a] *Men had first, long before others, arriv'd at the various beginnings of Religions* (as AMMIANUS MARCELLINUS speaks) *and that they preserv'd the first occasions of Sacred Rites conceal'd in their secret Writings:* yet I shall not trouble you with repeating the Arguments I have already produc'd to this purpose in *the History of the Soul's Immortality,*

[a] Hic primum Homines, longe ante alios, ad varia Religionum incunabula (ut dicitur) pervenerunt, & initia prima Sacrorum caute tuentur condita Scriptis arcanis. *Lib.* 22.

mortality, from the Authority of HERODOTUS, DIODORUS SICULUS, LUCIAN, DION CASSIUS, MACROBIUS, and others: nor will I urge that, by Examples and Laws from the Pentateuch, it clearly appears that Magick, the Interpretation of Dreams, Astrology, and Necromancy, were long us'd in Egypt before they were known in Chaldæa or any other place. Letter III.

2. THE most antient Egyptians, Persians, and Romans, the first Patriarchs of the Hebrews, with several other Nations and Sects, had no sacred Images or Statues, no peculiar Places or costly Fashions of Worship; the plain Easiness of their Religion being most agreeable to the Simplicity of the Divine Nature, as indifference of Place or Time were the best Expressions of infinite Power and Omnipresence. But tho *God did thus make Men upright, yet they found out* (says the wisest King of Israel) *many Inventions*. And certainly when once a Man suffers himself to be led into precarious or arbitrary Practices, he cannot stop for any Reason, but what, if it be good, must conclude with equal Force against all. I believe I Eccl. 7. 29.

Letter III. may without much difficulty prove, that such as first entertain'd Designs against the Liberty of Mankind, were also the first Depravers of their Reason. For none, in his right senses, can ever be persuaded voluntarily to part with his Freedom; and he that makes use of Force to deprive him of it, must have brib'd or deluded very many beforehand to support his unjust Pretensions, by which accession of strength he cou'd seduce, frighten, or subdue others. It will not therefore appear unlikely that Men very early learnt to have the same Conceptions of God himself, which they had before of their earthly Princes: and after thus fancying him mutable, jealous, revengeful, and arbitrary, they next endeavour'd to procure his Favor much after the same manner that they made their court to those who pretended to be his Representatives or Lieutenants, nay to be Gods themselves, or to be descended of heavenly Parentage, as the antient Monarchs us'd to do.

3. IT seems evident from the remotest Monuments of Learning, that all Superstition originally related to the Worship of the Dead, being principally deriv'd

deriv'd from Funeral Rites, tho the first occasion might be very innocent or laudable, and was no other than Orations wherein they were somtimes personally addrest (such as the Panegyricks of the Egyptians) or Statues dedicated with many Ceremonys to their Memory. But the Flatterers of great Men in the Persons of their Predecessors, the excessive Affection of Friends or Relations, and the Advantage which the Heathen Priests drew from the Credulity of the simple, carry'd this matter a great deal further. Not only Kings and Queens, great Generals and Legislators, the Patrons of Learning, Promoters of curious Arts, and Authors of useful Inventions, partook of this Honor; but also such private Persons, as by their virtuous Actions had distinguish'd themselves from others, were often consecrated to pious and eternal Memory by their Country or their Kindred, as reputable to the Dead, and exemplary to the Living. This is the true reason (as we shall shew in its proper place) of all Nations having their proper ‡ tutelary Gods; and hence Letter III.

‡ Divi Indigetes.

are

Letter III. are deriv'd the peculiar Religions of * particular Familys. PLINY, † in the second Book of his *Natural History*, says, That *the most antient way of Mens paying their Acknowledgments to their Benefactors, was by deifying of them after their Decease* (which was affirm'd by ‡ CICERO with several others before him) *and that the several Appellations of the Gods and of the Stars are deriv'd from the meritorious Actions of Men.* The first Idolatry therefore did not proceed (as 'tis commonly suppos'd) from the Beauty, or Order, or Influence of the Stars; but Men, as I told you in *the History of the Soul's Immortality*, observing Books to perish by Fire, Worms, or Rottenness; and Iron, Brass, or Marble not less subject to violent Hands or the Injurys of the Weather, they impos'd on the Stars (as the only

* Sacra Gentilitia.

† Hic est vetustissimus referendi bene merentibus Gratiam mos, ut tales Numinibus adscribant: quippe & omnium aliorum nomina Deorum, & quæ supra retuli Syderum, ex hominum nata sunt meritis.

‡ Suscepit autem vita Hominum consuetudoque communis, ut beneficiis excellentes viros in Coelum fama ac voluntate tollerent; hinc Hercules, hinc Castor & Pollux, &c. *De Nat. Deor. l.* 2.

everlasting Monuments) the proper Names of their Heroes, or of something memorable in their History. ERATOSTHENES the Cyrenean, a very antient Philosopher of prodigious Knowledg in all the Sciences, wrote a Book (yet extant) *of the Constellations*, wherein he delivers the Reasons of their Names, which are perpetual Allusions to antient History, tho wonderfully disguiz'd by Time, and for the most part mere Fables. The most learned Monsieur LE CLERC, when he wrote an Extract of ERATOSTHENES, among some other Mythological Tracts in the eighth Volume of *the Universal and Historical Library*, made the following Epigram.

Letter III.

: *Antiquity, b'ing sure that Nature's Force*
Wou'd Brass and Marble Monuments consume,
Did wisely its own History transmit
To future Times by Heav'ns eternal Fires.

: Tempore, cum lapidum sciret monumenta vetustas,
Atque perire suo cuncta metalla situ;
Cauta, suam, ætates fertur docuisse futuras
Cælorum æternis ignibus, Historiam.

In

Letter III.

In other places he declares himself to be of the same opinion concerning the Appellations of the Stars, and in that very Journal explains some Fables upon this Principle. As divers Nations learnt this Custom one of another, so they accordingly chang'd their Spheres, each imposing on the heavenly Bodys the Names and Actions belonging to their own Country. This is manifest in the Spheres of the Greeks and Barbarians, and for this reason the Cretans maintain'd that *most of the Gods were born among them, being Men, who, for their Benefits to the Publick, had obtain'd immortal Honors*[1]: for they believ'd the Grecian Gods to be those of all Mankind, and knew not that in other places this way of naming the Constellations and deifying deserving Men, was long in use before they had practis'd it. Nor was there wanting one among the Christians, who, approving this Method, endeavour'd to abolish those

---

[1] Τῶν θεῶν δὲ τοὺς πλείστους μυθολογοῦσι παρ' ἑαυτοῖς γεγονέναι, τοὺς διὰ τὰς κοινὰς εὐεργεσίας τυχόντας ἀθανάτων τιμῶν. Diod. Sic. l. 5.

Heathen

Heathen Names, as not understood, or of no concern to us; and to impose on the Stars new Names in their stead, containing the History of the Old and New Testament. But since he cou'd not prevail with the Astronomers, let's not digress. At last such as were ignorant or asham'd of the true Reasons of these things, wou'd justify their Worship (tho, as I shall evince, by weak Arguments) from the endless and orderly Revolution, the admirable Lustre, and general Usefulness of the Sun, Moon, and other Planets and Stars. This did likewise give the Philosophers a handle to explain the Motions of the Planets by certain Intelligences fixt and inhabiting in their Orbs, which they perpetually guided in their Courses; and hence the Bodys of the Sun and Moon are painted like a Face with Eyes, Nose, and a Mouth.

4. THE Opinion of the twelve greater Gods proceeded from certain Historys affix'd to the twelve Signs of the Zodiack, as the seven Planets bear the Names of as many Persons, to whom were also consecrated the Days of the Week, but reputed more or less holy,

Letter III.

5. SINCE thus I have accounted for Magick and judiciary Astrology, I shall, before I go any further, add a word or two about Peoples looking up when they pray, believing Heaven to be over their Heads, and Hell under their Feet. I shall likewise produce the occasional Causes of Ghosts and Specters: for all those Things came from the same common Root with the Origin of Idolatry, that is, from the Rites of the Antients about dead Bodys. In the Letter about *the Immortality of the Soul among the Heathens*, I explain'd to you by what Degrees the People came to be persuaded that there were Persons living in the Stars; and here I'll show you how they arriv'd to the supreme Dignity of Godship: from which you'l easily perceive that this introduc'd the Custom of Mens lifting up their Eyes, and extending their Hands to Heaven when they pray, directing themselves to the Gods whom they beheld above them. From the same Funeral Rites they believ'd Hell to be under them, and to be the Mansion of the Good and the Bad, tho distinguish'd in their Places

Letter III. and Conditions; becauſe all ſorts of Men were equally bury'd, and only a ſmaller number deify'd, whom they thought to be above: whereas in the Univerſe, properly ſpeaking, there is in reality neither Above nor Below, Right nor Left, Eaſt, Weſt, North, or South, theſe being only abſtracted Notions, denoting the Relations of particular Bodys to one another, and their ſeveral Situations in reſpect of us. The Fancy of Ghoſts and Specters proceeded in like manner from the Egyptian Mummys, theſe being ſo long kept intire, not only in the Grots near Memphis, but alſo by many People in fine Apartments at home, and which (whether preſerving their Lineaments freſh, or becoming ghaſtly with Time) cou'd naturally make frightful Impreſſions on Children, Strangers, and the ignorant Vulgar. Tho Humation, or the placing of the intire Corps under Ground, was the moſt antient and univerſal manner of Burial, and that the Athenians are acknowledg'd to have learn'd it of the Egyptians, yet you know the Romans were accuſtom'd to burn their dead Bodys; and nevertheleſs, as CICERO judiciouſly remarks, they

they were nothing cur'd thereby of their Notions concerning Ghoſts and Spectres, Humation having bin likewiſe their firſt Method of Burial. *And ſo prevalent was Error,* [1] ſays he, *that tho they knew the Bodys were burnt, yet they feign'd ſuch things to be tranſacted in the infernal Places, which without Bodys can neither be done nor underſtood: For as they cou'd not frame any Notion in their Minds of Souls living in a ſeparate State, so they ſought out ſome Form or Figure. Thence proceeded all* HOMER's *Divination by the Dead; thence thoſe necromantick Rites which my Friend* APPIUS *us'd to perform; thence in our Neighbourhood the Lake of* Avernus,

Letter III.

Whence Ghoſts are nightly rais'd, and
Gates of deepeſt Hell

---

[1] Tantumque valuit Error—ut corpora cremata cum ſcirent, tamen ea fieri apud inferos fingerent, quæ ſine corporibus nec fieri poſſent nec intelligi. Animos enim per ſeipſos viventes non poterant mente complecti, Formam aliquam Figuramque quærebant. Inde Homeri tota Νεκυια: inde ea quæ meus amicus Appius Νεκρομαντια faciebat: inde in Vicinia noſtra Averni Lacus,

Unde Animæ excitantur obſcura umbra, aperto oſtio
Alti Acherontis, falſo ſanguine imagines mortuorum.

Tuſc. Quæſt. l. 1.

Letter III.

Open to false Bodys, Images of the Dead.

6. THUS you see, MADAM, how they took care to people Hell; and the truth is, that the very Heaven of the Gentiles was wholly inhabited by Colonys from our Earth. CICERO in his first [1] *Tusculan Disputation*, boldly says, *Is not all Heaven full of human Race? If I shou'd be at the pains of searching among the Antients, and particularly the Greek Writers, those, who are accounted the principal Gods, will be found to have remov'd from among us into Heaven. Ask whose are the Sepulchers they show in Greece. Remember, seeing you are initiated, what is told at the Celebration of the Mysterys; and then you'll understand how very far this Business reaches.*

---

[1] Totum pene Cœlum nonne humano Genere completum est? Si vero scrutari vetera; & ex his ea quæ Scriptores Graci prodiderunt eruere coner; ipsi illi, majores gentium Dii qui habentur, hinc a nobis profecti in Cœlum reperientur. Quære quorum demonstrantur sepulchra in Græcia. Reminiscere, quoniam es initiatus, quæ traduntur Mysteriis; tum denique quam hoc late pateat intelliges.

Nor

Nor was it at the Eleusinian Mysterys only that such Discoverys were made, for those of the Egyptians adumbrated the Death of their deify'd King OSIRIS and his Queen ISIS; to speak nothing of the Syrian Rites in Honor of ADONIS and other Deitys, which King DAVID most properly calls *the Sacrifices of the Dead.* It is as true of all the Mysterys in general, what CICERO says in another place of those of Eleusis, Samothracia, and Lemnos, [1] *That being explain'd, and reduc'd to the Examination of Reason, the Nature of Things is better known than that of the Gods.* EUHEMERUS, an old Sicilian Poet and Philosopher, wrote the History of SATURN, JUPITER, and the rest of that sort, describing the Birth, Country, Actions, and Buryal-place of each; and, as PLUTARCH words it, [2] *He humaniz'd the Gods,* not transforming but reducing them to Men, such as they [3] truly were before. But, not con-

Letter III.

Psal. 106. 28.

[1] Quibus explicatis, ad rationemque revocatis, rerum magis natura cognoscitur quam Deorum. *De Nat. Deor. lib.* 1.

[2] Ἐξανθρωπίζει τὰ θεῖα.

[3] Ab Euhemero autem & Mortes & Sepulturæ demonstrantur Deorum. *Cic. de Nat. Deor. l.* 1.

Letter III. tent thus to deify the Dead, they assign'd them the same Inclinations and Offices which they had before on Earth, and, as VIRGIL sings of his Warriors,

> [1] *The same Delight they took alive in Arms,*
> *To course in Chariots, or breed stately Horses,*
> *With equal Care imploys their Ghosts below.*

So HESIOD, very pertinently to our purpose, represents the happy Inhabitants of the Golden Age like the most antient Princes, injoying their former Power above, and as being the Distributers of Riches and Honors here on Earth.

> [2] *These by great* JOVE's *Decree now Dæmons are,*

Ce-

---

[1] ——Quæ gratia curruum,
Armorumque fuit vivis, quæ cura nitentes
Pascere equos, eadem sequitur tellure repostos.
Æn. l. 6.

[2] Τοὶ μὲν Δαίμονές εἰσι Διὸς μεγάλου διὰ βουλὰς,
Ἐσθλοὶ,

Celestial, Good, Guardians of mortal Men, Letter III.
Observing all their just or wicked Deeds,
B'ing cloth'd with Air, and wandring o'er the Earth,
They Wealth and Honors to their Fav'rites give;
For still their kingly Office they retain.

From the same Spring the old Ethiopians, as we learn from STRABO, [a] *believ'd their Benefactors and Persons of royal Extract to be Gods*, and, no doubt, to benefit and protect them still from above, as they formerly us'd to do below.

7. I DON'T pretend, MADAM, that these false Notions of the Heathens about the Dead were the only Rise of Idolatry; but I maintain it was the first, the

---

Εσθλοι, επιχθονιοι, φυλακες θνητων ανθρωπων,
Οἱ ῥα φυλασσουσιν τε δικας και σχετλια εργα,
Ηερα εσσαμενοι, παντη φοιτωντες επ' αιαν,
Πλουτοδοται; και τουτο γερας βασιληιον εσχον.

Oper. & Dies.

[a] Ὡς δε επι το πολυ τους Ευεργετας και βασιλικους θεους νομιζουσι. Lib. 17.

Letter III. most natural, the most universal, and what gave occasion to all the rest. The same excessive Respect was transfer'd by degrees to other things, both as being the Gifts of the Gods, and for their own innate Excellency. [1] *There are many other Natures of the Gods*, says CICERO, *(not without reason, because of their great Benefits) instituted and nam'd by the wisest Men of Greece, and by our Ancestors: for whatever cou'd bring great profit to Mankind, that thing they thought cou'd not be made without the Divine Bounty towards Men.* But they did not restrain this Notion to those useful things without us, nor to the celestial Bodys; they also extended the like Privilege to the Dispositions of the Mind, to its Facultys, and Virtues: for, according to the same CICERO, [2] *The thing it self, in which there is any great worth, is so*

---

[1] Multæ autem aliæ naturæ Deorum ex magnis Beneficiis eorum, non sine causa, & a Græciæ sapientissimis & majoribus nostris constitutæ nominatæque sunt: quicquid enim magnam utilitatem generi afferret humano, id non sine divina Bonitate erga Homines fieri arbitrabantur. *De Nat. Deor. l.* 2.

[2] Tum autem res ipsa in quâ vis inest major aliqua sic

so term'd by them, that even this very Worth is call'd a God, as Fidelity, the Mind, &c. And so Virtue, Honor, Safety, Concord, Chastity, Liberty, Victory, Clemency, Piety, and such like, were deify'd; *in all which things*, adds he, ' *because there was so great a Worth that it could not be manag'd without God, the Thing it self has obtain'd the name of a God, of which kind the words Cupid and Desire, Venus and Love, are consecrated*. Without question, when wise and good Men perceiv'd that the People wou'd needs have a plurality of Gods, and Temples dedicated to them, they, to comply with their Weakness, and at the same time to bring 'em as much as they cou'd to better and nobler Thoughts, deify'd such Things. Hence may be perceiv'd how so many Things came to be deify'd, which have no personal Form or Existence, and are nothing else but mere

Letter III.

sic appellatur, ut ea ipsa vis nominetur Deus, ut Fides, ut Mens, &c. *Ibid.*

' Quarum omnium rerum quia vis erat tanta ut sine Deo regi non posset, ipsa res Deorum nomen obtinuit, quo ex genere Cupidinis & Voluntatis, & lubentinæ Veneris vocabula consecrata sunt. *Ibid.*

Propertys,

Letter III. Propertys, Modes, or Accidents. This made CICERO appoint in his Laws (a matter practis'd in Rome before) that those things shou'd be reputed Gods, [1] *for the sake of which Man was admitted to ascend into Heaven.— 'Tis well done,* says he, *that the Mind, Piety, Virtue, Faith, are consecrated, of all which the Temples are publickly dedicated at Rome; that those who have them (and all good Men have them) may think that the Gods themselves are plac'd in their Minds.*

8. BUT as the Superstitious pervert every thing in Heaven and Earth, so they fail'd not to do in this case, consecrating the most vitious and abominable things, for which our Author justly reprehends them. The Athenians were bless'd with a couple of fine Goddesses, Contumely and Impudence; the Romans had Fear and Hope, Paleness

[1] Propter quæ datur homini ascensus in Cœlum.—— Bene vero quod Mens, Pietas, Virtus, Fides, consecrantur manu, quarum omnium Romæ dedicata publice Templa sunt: ut illa qui habeant (habent autem omnes boni) Deos ipsos in Animis suis collocatos putent. *De Leg. l.* 2.

and

and Trembling. The destructive Fever had an Altar; and there was an endless rabble of Gods presiding over the foulest Distempers, and even over Actions very barbarous and obscene. The Egyptians, besides the Worship of the celestial Gods, or of the Stars and Planets, had withal a symbolical Worship on Earth, attributing Divine Virtues and paying a religious Respect to almost all sorts of Animals and Plants, not excepting the most vile and contemptible. Yet all parts of Egypt did not reverence the same Species. The Reasons they alledg'd in their own Justification, were either the Usefulness of these things, or that the several Deitys manifested their particular Powers more in one Species than in another, or they pretended to some Allegory drawn from Morality or Natural Philosophy. [1] *In their Sacred Rites,* says PLUTARCH, *there's nothing appointed that's unreasonable (as some imagine) or fabulous, or from Superstition; but some things*

---

[1] Ουδεν αλογον, ουδε μυθωδες, ουδε υπο Δεισιδαιμονιας (ωσπερ ενιοι νομιζουσιν) εγκατεστοιχειωτο ιερουργιαις: αλλα

Letter III.

things having moral and useful Causes, and others not being void of some historical or philosophical Elegance. Agreeable to which Cicero says, that *the very Egyptians,* [1] *who are so much laught at, have not consecrated any Beast, but for some Advantage that they drew from it.* This symbolical Theology made several learned Men believe that all the other parts of the Heathen Religions might and ought to be so explain'd, which I shall prove to be a great mistake before I have done. The Egyptians indeed carry'd it farther than all others: for they did not only worship the Bird Ibis, Hawks, Cats, Dogs, Crocodiles, Sea-horses, Goats, Bulls, Cows, Onions, Garlick, and what not? but [2] *they worshipt a Man in the Town of Anubis, in which they sacrific'd to him, and burnt the sacred stuff on the Altars.*

αλλα τα μεν ηθικας εχοντα και χρειωδεις αιτιας, τα δε ουκ αμοιρα κομψοτητος ιστορικης η φυσικης εστιν. De Iside & Osiride.

[1] Ipsi illi, qui irridentur, Ægyptii, nullam Belluam, nisi ob aliquam utilitatem quam ex ea caperent, consecraverunt. *De Nat. Deor. l.* 1.

[2] Ανθρωπον σεβουσιν κατα Ανουβιν κωμην, εν ῃ και τυτω θυεται, και επι των βωμων τα ιερεια καεται. De Abstin. l. 4.

They

They are the words of PORPHYRY. Letter III.

9. IN other Countrys some paid a philosophical Worship to the four Elements, and certain parts of the human Body. Other Citys as well as that of Rome were elevated to the high Dignity of Goddesses. And many for fear of offending by mistake erected Altars to [1] unknown Gods. The Romans frankly naturaliz'd those of all other Nations, falling down before such Deitys as cou'd not protect their antient Votarys from the Power of their Arms: yet this was rather a politick Liberty of Conscience, than the Effects of any real Devotion. Now from all this it is very evident, not only that the Gods did infinitely exceed Mankind in number as well as in dignity; but that, tho Superstition cou'd be kept within no bounds, yet all Idolatry had its Original from mens Notions and Actions about dead Bodys. But no Absurdity seems greater to me than to find Divinity attributed to Chance, which is directly

[1] Diog. Laert. in Epimenide. Pausan. in Attic. & Lucian. in Philopat.

opposite

Letter III. opposite to all Order, Intelligence, and Design: and, nevertheless, under the name of Fortune it had its proper Temples, one dedicated to good, and another to bad Fortune; at the same time receiving Divine Worship, and the most opprobrious Epithets of blind, various, inconstant, true to the worst, and a jilt to the best. These things, as in the Sequel will appear, were introduc'd and invented at second hand; but all occasion'd and grounded on the Worship of the Dead.

10. I AM far from designing to bring all the Arguments I cou'd to demonstrate my Opinion about *the Origin of Idolatry*, yet I cannot forbear producing one Example, which shows the utmost Extravagance of human Nature. Tho the generality of Christians have almost made a Martyr of SOCRATES as dying for the Belief of one God, and that the Heathens will have his guilt to have bin for introducing other Gods than the State allow'd, yet both these Assertions are false: for to his death he adher'd to the Worship of his Country, being of opinion that no private Person ought to separate

separate from the publick Establishment; and tho he might believe but one God, yet this was none of the Crimes objected to him by his Accusers or his Judges. However, considering the Sentiments of all Men about him, it seems scarce credible that this Father of good Manners, this Prince of Philosophers, and ablest Physician of the Mind, shou'd have divine Honors paid to himself after his death, that he shou'd have a Temple and a Fountain dedicated to his Name. We read, it's true, that the Athenians, repenting of their injust Sentence, and to acknowledg his exemplary worth, erected a Statue to perpetuate his Memory: and we know (what is very natural) that his Admirers celebrated his Birth-day, and wore the Figure of his Head about them on Gems in their Rings or Seals. But this Veneration at last was carry'd to religious Worship. For MARINUS, the Disciple and Successor of PROCLUS at Athens, who wrote his Master's Life, and who speaks of a thing he knew as well as I do to what Saint my Parish-Church is dedicated: MARINUS, I say, relating the happy Presages of PROCLUS's succeeding in the Platonick School, says, that

Letter III.

Letter III. that [1] *as he arriv'd at the Piræum,* NICOLAS, *who afterwards grew famous in the Art of Declamation, but study'd then under the Professors at Athens, went down to the Port as to one of his Acquaintance, to receive and lodg him as his Countryman; for* NICOLAS *was likewise a Lycian, and so he conducted him into the City. But* (PROCLUS) *finding himself weary after his Voyage, sat down by the way in the Chappel of* SOCRATES (*when as yet he neither knew nor had heard that* SOCRATES *was honor'd in any place thereabouts*) *and pray'd* NICOLAS *that he wou'd likewise sit down a little, and, if he cou'd any where, to help him to some Water. The other obeying him, order'd some to be brought*

[1] Ὡς γὰρ εἰς τὸν Πειραιᾶ κατῆρε, Νικόλαος, ὁ ὕστερον μὲν περιφανὴς ἐπὶ τῇ σοφιστικῇ γενόμενος, τηνικαῦτα δὲ σχολάζων τοῖς ἐν Ἀθήναις Διδασκάλοις, κάτεισιν εἰς τὸν Λιμένα, ὡς πρὸς γνώριμον, ὑποδεξάμενός τε αὐτὸν καὶ ξεναγήσων εἰς πόλιν. Λύκιος γὰρ καὶ ὁ Νικόλαος. Ἦγεν οὖν αὐτὸν ἐπὶ τὴν πόλιν. Ὁ δὲ ἐκ τῆς βαδίσεως κόπου ᾔσθετο κατὰ τὴν Ὁδὸν, καὶ περὶ τὸ Σωκράτειον, οὔπω εἰδὼς οὐδὲ ἀκηκοὼς ὅτι Σωκράτους αὐτοῦ τι ἐγίγνοντο τιμαί· ἠξίου δὲ τὸν Νικόλαον ἐπιμεῖναι τε αὐτόθι βραχὺ, καὶ καθέζεσθαι, ἅμα δὲ καὶ εἰ ἔχοι ποθὲν ὕδωρ αὐτῷ πορίσασθαι: καὶ γὰρ δίψει πολλῷ, ὡς ἔλεγεν, κατείχετο. Ὁ δὲ ἕτοιμος αὐτῷ, καὶ τοῦτο οὐκ ἀλλαχόθεν ποθὲν,

ἐξ

brought immediately, and that from no other place, but from that same consecrated Ground: for the Fountain of Socrates's *Statue was not far from thence. Now, as he was drinking,* Nicolas, *who thought of it only just then, said to him, this is a good Omen that you have sat in the Temple of* Socrates, *and that there you drunk the first Attic Water. Then* Proclus, *rising up and worshipping, proceeded on his way to the City.* Here you have an Example in all Forms how the Veneration of dead Men becomes excessive in time; and I have chosen to relate it thus at length, because it was most unlikely to happen to Socrates, tho more deserving it than any other.

Letter III.

11. I SHOU'D never have done, SERENA, if I wou'd confirm my Opinion by all the Authoritys I cou'd

---

ἐξ αὐτȣ δὲ ἐκείνȣ τȣ ἱερȣ χωρίȣ ἐποίει φέρεσθαι· ȣδὲ γὰρ πόῤῥω ἦν ἡ πηγὴ τῆς Σωκράτȣς στήλης. Πίοντι δὲ αὐτῷ σύμβολον ὁ Νικόλαος, τότε πρῶτον ἐπιστήσας, εἶπεν, ὡς τῷ Σωκρατείῳ εἴη ἐνιδρυθεὶς, καὶ πρῶτον ἐκεῖθεν Ἀττικὸν ὕδωρ πιών. Ὁ δὲ, ἐξαναστὰς καὶ προσκυνήσας, ἐπὶ τὴν πόλιν ἐπορεύετο. Marin. in vita Procli, Cap. 10. Edit. Lond.

Letter III. produce. Whoever is conversant in the Learning of the Antients, and considers the Accounts they have left us of their own Original as well as that of other Nations, what they have particularly written of their Gods, and the Reasons of their Deification, can have no doubts remaining concerning this matter. But 'tis observable, that according to the degrees of Improvement any Nation made in Politeness, Literature, or Government, the less they were addicted to this impious Humor of God-making. To give an Instance hereof, the Romans deify'd ROMULUS their first King and Founder; but, during those many hundred Years their Commonwealth subsisted, they did not consecrate one Mortal, tho for Virtue, Knowledg, and Valor, they were furnish'd with more deserving Examples than all the World besides. And yet as soon as ever their free Republick was turn'd into absolute Monarchy, the greatest part of the first Emperors were deify'd; both JULIUS CÆSAR the Subverter of their Liberty, and the most cruel, leud, or foolish of the succeeding Tyrants, with some of their Wives, Relations, and Favorites; imitating

imitating herein the Custom of Kings among the Barbarians, who by such Artifices kept their Subjects in perpetual Slavery, as not daring to rebel against the Gods, or those that were in Election to become such. There's nothing better known in History, than that Princes had Divine Honors paid 'em after Death by the Egyptians, Assyrians, the most antient Greeks, and other Nations. Their Queens also, their Brothers, Sisters, and other Kindred, were made Gods and Goddesses; and it was always the Interest of the succeeding Monarch, to keep up this extraordinary Notion of his Race. Nay Divine Worship was offer'd to many others during their Lives, as well as to AUGUSTUS. PLUTARCH, to whom I might add several more Authors, relates that ARTABANUS, a Persian Lord, said to THEMISTOCLES, then a Fugitive in that Court, [a] *Of the many and good Laws which we have, this is the most excellent, to honor*

Letter III.

---

[a] Ἡμῖν δὲ πολλῶν νόμων καὶ καλῶν ὄντων καλλιστος οὗτος ἐστι, τὸ τιμᾶν βασιλέα, καὶ προσκυνεῖν εἰκόνα Θεοῦ. In Themistocle.

Letter III. *the King, and to worship the Image of God.* No body is ignorant how sacred the Ottoman Race is esteem'd; tho this, as we see, cannot always preserve 'em from the Fury of their insolent Guards or of their injur'd Subjects. The Divine Right claim'd of late by some Christian Kings, and the unreserv'd and passive Obedience pretended by their flattering Clergy to be due to them, if not a better Expedient to support Tyranny than that of the Heathens, yet they were unquestionably intended for the same end and purpose. But the wiser Men grew, the less they believ'd of these things; on the contrary the more narrowly they watch'd their Princes, the more jealous they became of their Liberty and Privileges. Religion and Reason are hated Obstacles to Superstition and Error; and CICERO remarks that some Oracles ceas'd to give Responses in his time, because People were grown less credulous.

12. HAVING hitherto explain'd and establish'd the Origin of Idolatry, I shall now, MADAM, conformably to these Principles, assign the Reasons of

of the Heathen Rites, if you'l allow any Reason to be given for Practices in many cases very absurd and extravagant. Men thinking to please their God (whoever he was among so many) as they were wont to do while a Prince on Earth, erected magnificent Temples or Palaces, and on sumptuous Tables or Altars they made Feasts or Sacrifices to him; imagining that he and his Court (principally compos'd of their deceas'd Heroes) did feed on the Blood and Fumes of slaughter'd Animals, and delight their celestial Nostrils with snuffing up the Fragrancy of Incense, as they did their sacred Eyes with Pomp and Shows. All the Attendance was sutable to their State and Dignity when living. Solemn Times or Holy-days were set apart from ordinary Labor for the Celebration of the Feast; and those, whom afterwards they call'd their Priests (whose business was to order the Feast, to serve the Company, and to repeat a Panegyrick in Commemoration of the deify'd Mortal) were clad in splendid Garments, and endow'd with several commodious Privileges, as the Servants of Princes always are: but the chiefest at the beginning

Letter III.

Letter III. ginning were an Exemption from every other Duty to the Publick, and plentiful Salarys assign'd for their Livelihood. There was likewise at these Feasts, good store of Musick, Dancing, Perfuming, Illuminations, Bowings, Cringings, Prostrations, and every thing besides that is usually imploy'd to gratify the Senses of the most vain or licentious Prince; but cou'd never be thought acceptable to any Divine Being, without placing the Origin of Idolatry in the Worship of the Dead, which makes such Worship and Ceremonys very accountable.

13. AS they did with the Ministers of their Princes, so they must make an Interest both with the Courtiers in Heaven and with the Priests on Earth; not only bribing them for their Intercession, but if they wou'd not favor, at least not to oppose their Petitions: for they were commonly of different Factions above as well as below. But you must understand that the Power of these Courtiers was of no small moment, the Government and Protection of all Regions and Citys, particularly of those where they liv'd or govern'd themselves, being dis-

tributed

tributed among 'em. There was neither Tree nor Plant; nor Beast, Fish, or Fowl; nor River, Fountain, nor Hill; nor almost any other Creature, but was the special Care and Delight of one or other of them, and frequently call'd after their Names, as in their Life-time they happen'd to use, or love, or admire them. This immediate Direction they were thought to have on the Things now mention'd, as well as over the Diseases of the Body and the Passions of the Mind, gave a Reputation and Authority to their pretended Miracles, Apparitions, Divinations, Oracles, and all other Arts of the Cunning, to drain the Pockets of the Credulous.

Letter III.

14. AS for the Sanctuarys and the secret Arks kept in them, with their many mysterious Doings, their Expiations, Purifications, and other ridiculous, profane, or cruel Ceremonys, and all very burdensom; these, I say, were at the beginning symbolical, representing the true History of the Gods while living on Earth, exhibiting the Reasons of their Deification, and the Arks in particular containing the Emblems, Marks, or Tokens of the whole Fact, as all a-

gree who have look'd into the Heathen Myſterys. But theſe things were afterwards manag'd by the Prieſts ſo as to make their imagin'd Intimacy with Heaven more valu'd, and to get Revenues ſettled on themſelves, proportionable to the Laboriouſneſs and Importance of the Service in which they were engag'd. Nor did the Multitude of the Rites ſerve a little to amuſe and diſtract the Vulgar from reflecting on matters with more conſideration, their whole Time being almoſt employ'd about them: beſides that they muſt needs entertain a high Opinion of them, who cou'd affix Sanctity to Times, Places, and Perſons, and to ſuch things as were either indifferent in their own Natures, or ſeem'd the fartheſt imaginable from being religious. Moreover, there was not wanting ſometimes a mutual Compact between the Prince and the Prieſt, whereby the former oblig'd himſelf to ſecure all theſe Advantages to the latter, if he in return would preach up his abſolute Power over the People, on whoſe well-meaning Underſtandings he cou'd make what Impreſſions he pleas'd at any time.

Letter III.

15. TO the Authority of Princes they added their own Inventions about Hell (as I show'd before in this Letter, and also in the last I sent you) not contenting themselves to terrify Men with Ice and Flames, deep Mire and Darkness, *they added Vultures, Rolling-Stones, Wheels, and Chains; Hydras, Centaurs, Harpies, Chimeras, Sphynxes, Gorgons, Dragons, and a World of other Monsters, the Executioners of the Princes Tyranny. They told 'em also of Ghosts and Specters, Visions and Voices, amazing the Vulgar with the tremendous Sounds of Tartarus, Erebus, the black and roaring Waves of

Styx, Acheron, Phlegethon, Lethe, Cocytus, Avernus;

with the hideous barking of triple-headed CERBERUS, the dogged Sullenness of CHARON the Ferryman: but the inexorable Furys, ALECTO, TISIPHONE, and MEGÆRA, were more dreaded by far than PLUTO or PROSERPINA, tho Sovereign Governors over those infernal Regions. From

Letter III. From what I said before about the Origin of Ghosts and Astrology, you may be sure they were addicted to all manner of Divination and Magick, such as [1] Augurys and Auspicys, [2] Extispicys, [3] Necromancy and Necyomancy, [4] Pyromancy, [5] Psychomancy, [6] Nephelomancy, [7] Hydromancy, [8] Capnomancy, [9] Sortileges, with other numberless and superstitious Vanitys, which are continu'd in most parts of the World to this very Time, and which may be found describ'd at large in VANDALE. We may imagin, from the same Reasons, that they abounded with Witches, Sorcerers, and Fortune-tellers, who, by virtue of a Covenant or [10] Compact with the Dæmons, by their Knowledg of the

[1] *Divining by Birds and Signs.* [2] *By the Entrals of Animals.* [3] *By the Dead and Ghosts.* [4] *By Fire.* [5] *By Souls.* [6] *By the Clouds.* [7] *By Water.* [8] *By Smoak.* [9] *By Lots, whether in Passages of Books or otherwise.*

[10] Quis labor hic superis, Cantus Herbasque sequendi
Spernendiq; Timor? Cujus Commercia PACTI
Obstrictos habuere Deos? Parere necesse est,
An juvat? Ignota tantum pietate merentur,
An tacitis valuere minis? Hoc Juris in omnes
Est illis superos? An habent hæc Carmina certum
Imperiosa Deum, qui Mundum cogere, quicquid
Cogitur ipse, potest? *Lucan. Pharsal. l. 6.*

Stars,

Stars, and by the occult Qualitys of certain Herbs, Stones, barbarous Words, and Charms, and by pricking, or melting, or burying the Images of the Partys concern'd, pretended to make the Gods appear, and to raise the Ghosts of the Dead; to darken the Sun and Moon, and make the Planets more backward, nay to bring down the Stars from the Firmament; to transform themselves and others into various Shapes; to afflict whom they pleas'd with Distempers; procure Love or Hatred; foretel future Events; discover hidden Treasures; spirit away Peoples Corn, or Milk, or other Goods; change little Children in their Cradles; and a thousand more such Pranks, tedious to relate, and impossible for thinking Men to believe. But what the Learned and the Prudent thought of all these Pretenders to extraordinary Knowledg, old ENNIUS will frankly tell you in his rugged Measures.

Letter III.

[1] *I value not one rush a Marsian Augur,*

Nor

[1] Non habeo denique nauci Marsum Augurem,

Non

Letter III.

Nor Country Fortunetellers, nor Town Star-gazers,
Nor Jugling-Gypsies, nor yet Dream-Interpreters:
For not by Skill or Art are these Diviners;
But superstitious Prophets, Guessers impudent,
Or idle Rogues, or craz'd, or mere starving Beggars.
They know no way themselves, yet others would direct;
And crave a Groat of those, to whom they promise Riches,
Thence let 'em take the Groat, and give back all the rest.

We may add here the fabulous Storys of the Heathens (much like our modern Tales of Fairys) concerning their Sylvans, Fauns and Satyrs; their Larvæ

Non vicanos Aruspices, non de circo Astrologos,
Non Isiacos Conjectores, non Interpretes Somnium:
Non enim sunt ii aut scientia aut arte Divini,
Sed superstitiosi Vates, impudentesq; Harioli,
Aut inertes, aut insani, aut quibus Egestas imperat;
Qui sibi semitam non sapiunt, alteri monstrant viam,
Quibus divitias pollicentur ab iis Drachmam ipsi petunt,
De his divitiis sibi deducant Drachmam, reddant cætera. *Cic. de Divinat. lib.* 1.

and

and Lemures; their Nymphs of the Seas, Rivers, Fountains, Hills, and Woods, such as the Nereids, Naiads, Dryads, Hamadryads, Oreads, and if there be any more like to these, only fit to scare Women and Children.

Letter III.

16. LET's now return, if you please, to the higher Powers; for as in Life so after Death they were of several Orders, Gods of the upper, and Gods of the lower Form, the [1] Nobility and [2] Commons, as also [3] intermediate, inferior, and vagabond Dæmons (originally from the Supposition of departed Souls) who had no certain Habitation, but wander'd in the Air, and were constantly sent on Errands, either to carry the Prayers of Men to their Superiors, or to acquaint the World with the Wrath or Favor of the Gods, whereof they were commonly thought to be the Ministers and Executioners, for those Princes had their Armys in Heaven as well as on Earth. But as the

[1] Dii majorum Gentium.
[2] Dii minorum Gentium.
[3] Dii medioxumi, &c.

Hea-

Letter III. Heathens ſent the beſt of their Gods to Heaven, ſo they recall'd 'em again at their Pleaſure, confining their Preſence to ſome ſmall Chappel, or to the poor Idol within that: for they imagin'd that many of them liv'd in Tombs or wander'd in the Air, before they help'd 'em to thoſe Accommodations, where the Deſires of their Petitioners were more agreeably heard than in any other place. They often fell down before the Work of their own Hands, which, had it Life or Reflection, ought rather to worſhip them from whoſe Skill all its Excellency had bin deriv'd: but the wiſer Mice, Swallows, and Spiders made very bold with their Statues, notwithſtanding the virtue of Conſecration, while ſilly Men were forc'd themſelves to protect what they fear'd and ador'd. Theſe very Statues are an Argument of their human Figure and Original, and we know the reſpect that was paid to the Statues, even of living Princes. Their Shrines were often viſited by the moſt ignorant and devout, who alſo hung the Temples round with Offerings and rich Preſents, conſulted the Oracles in all dubious Events, bound themſelves by Vows in their Diſtreſs, believ'd their

their very Dreams to be divinely inspir'd, and made their Religion in every respect as troublesom to others as to themselves. From what they practis'd on Earth, there was not a darling Passion or Game of their great Men (such as drinking, wenching, or hunting) but the like were ascrib'd to the Gods. Wherefore we often read of their Amours, Marriages, Rapes and Adulterys; their Dissensions, Revellings, Quarrels, and Wounds; their Revenges and Thefts; their Complaints and manifold Distresses, being sometimes expos'd, at other times imprison'd, and once fairly beaten out of their Cittadel in Heaven by the Giants, to seek in a pitiful manner for shelter on Earth; all which things demonstrate their Earthly Original. We need not wonder after this to find, that they are always represented in the State wherein they dy'd, and with all the distinguishing Marks in which they liv'd. Thus are some of 'em ever old, and others ever young; Parents, Children, and Relations; some lame and blind, of different Colours and Appetites; some cloven-footed (whence the present vulgar notion of the Devil) some furnish'd with

Letter III.

Letter III. with Wings, or arm'd with Swords, Spears, Helmets, Clubs, Forks and Bows; or drawn in their Chariots by Lions, Tygers, Horses, Sea-calfs, Peacocks, and Doves. Now all these things were partly borrow'd from their true History, and are partly allegorical, poetical, and fabulous Disguises of what is no longer perfectly known nor understood.

17. ÆNOMAUS, EUHEMERUS, LUCIAN, and many other Persons who made use of their Reason, did fearlesly mock the Deitys for being naturaliz'd of this or that Place, where they exercis'd every one the Trade wherein he excell'd. Thus APOLLO had an Office of Intelligence, and told Fortunes at Delphos; ESCULAPIUS set up an Apothecary's Shop at Pergamus; VENUS kept a noted Baudyhouse at Paphos; VULCAN had a Blacksmith's Forge in Lemnos; some were Midwives, some Huntresses, and all of them traffick'd where they cou'd: for they us'd, like us Mortals, such as they had formerly bin, when they did not thrive in one place, to remove into some other more convenient

for

for their Businefs. As all Events were believ'd to be the Effects of their Love or Difpleafure, fo Men found out feveral Methods to thank or appeafe them; and particularly gave 'em (by way of acknowledgment for the reft) the Firft-Fruits of all Productions, whether of Animals or Vegetables, with Tythes and other Offerings which they were bound to pay to their Living Princes. Nor was there any thing almoft that came amifs in their Sacrifices; for what was the averfion of one prov'd the delight of another, and fome of 'em would be content with nothing under human Victims, an Argument of their bloody Difpofition in this World. We often find them highly refenting the Affront (as Princes and Great Men ufe to do) when their Altars were neglected, efpecially if the People feafted other Gods; and Men have not lefs frequently in their Turns reproach'd the Divine Powers with Ingratitude, and even outrag'd their Statues (being fometimes inclin'd to Rebellion) when they thought themfelves not fufficiently requited for the rich Prefents or Bribes which they gave them.

Letter III.

Letter III.

18. BUT tho the more learned and virtuous had many times better Notions of Things, yet we find the Sentiments of some of 'em mighty fluctuating and obscure, principally occasion'd by the Persecution that was sure to attend the Truth, or any attempt towards a general Reformation, witness the Death of SOCRATES. We may observe from [1] PLUTARCH, that the true Reason why the Theory of the Stars and Planets was so little, or at least not so generally known, was, that the common People wou'd never endure to hear those things made subject to a Philosophical Examination, or explain'd by the ordinary Laws of Nature, by involuntary Causes, and blind Facultys, while they held 'em to be intelligent, eternal, and immortal Gods. And therefore when ANAXAGORAS discover'd that the Moon had but a bor-

[1] Ουδ' ὁ λογος ἐνδοξος ἠν, αλλ' αποῤῥητος ετι και δι' ολιγων, και μετ' ευλαβειας τινος η πιστεως βαδιζων; ου γαρ ηνειχοντο τους φυσικους και μετεωρολεσχας τοτε καλουμενους, ὡς εις αιτιας αλογους και δυναμεις απρονοητους, και κατηναγκασμενα παθη, διατριβοντος το θειον. In vita Niciæ.

row'd

row'd Light from the Sun, and so gave the Reasons of its Wax and Wane, such a Doctrine durst not be made publick, but was secretly communicated to very few, and even to them under a Promise of Fidelity. Indeed a great many eminent Persons in Europe and Asia, both understood themselves the Origin of the Religions commonly receiv'd, and sometimes have dar'd to discover their Vanity, Insufficiency, and Imposture to others. But such as at any time thus asserted the Unity of the Deity, and expos'd Superstition, we ought not to reckon for Heathens, by which Expression is properly understood Idolaters who believe a plurality of Gods, and that pretend to have particular Revelations from them, with several sorts of Rites instituted to their Honor as they were thought to act in distinct Provinces, or else to commemorate their particular Actions. The Jews (who thought all the People of the World, but themselves, to be of this kind) usually call'd 'em the Nations, from the Greek whereof we have the word Heathens, and Gentiles from the Latin. All those therefore who had Penetration enough to discover, and Courage to oppose

Letter III.

Letter III. poſe the Folly or Craft of this Theology, were call'd and reputed Atheiſts; and treated as ſuch by the Multitude at the Inſtigation of the Prieſts. Several Perſons, eſpecially among the Philoſophers, were fin'd and impriſon'd, ſome were ſent into Exile, others judicially ſentenc'd to Death; many torn in pieces by the Rabble, and all of them conſtantly branded with Impiety for disbelieving the Myſterys, or expoſing the Holy Cheats of their Times. But no thanks are due to the Heathen Prieſts, that fewer Inſtances of this kind occur among them than the Chriſtians: for, beſides that moſt of the Heathen Prieſts differ'd little from Civil Magiſtrates, and that many of them did not continue in their Office for Life, they were likewiſe in perfect ſubjection to the State: whereas the Chriſtian Prieſts (except in a very few Proteſtant Countrys) overtop the Government, and are every where abſolute Maſters of the Underſtanding of the Laity. In our Diſcourſes therefore of the Antients, we are to aſcribe their ſound Notions or moral Practices to the Light of Reaſon, whereof Heatheniſm was a notorious Corruption. For want of obſerving this Diſtinction,

tinction, there are infinite Mistakes committed. One rashly maintains that Heathenism was a better Foundation for Virtue than Christianity, whereas he ought to have said no more (at most) than that the Law of Nature was often better fulfill'd by Heathens than Christians. Another thinks all those to have bin Idolaters who liv'd when Heathenism prevail'd, than which there cannot be a grosser Error. Can any Man be so stupid as to count CICERO (for example) a Heathen, who, in his admirable Treatises *of Divination* and *of the Nature of the Gods*, has demonstratively subverted their Polytheism, Sacrifices, pretended Revelations, Prophecys, and Miracles; their Oracles, Augurys, Oneirocriticks, Incantations, and all Fopperys of the like sort? MINUTIUS FELIX, TERTULLIAN, and other Primitive Apologists for Christianity, transcrib'd their best Arguments against Heathenism out of these and the like Books, and very often in the same words. ARNOBIUS, after doing Justice to others, maintains,

Letter III. maintains, that if [1] TULLY's Works were read, the Christians need not trouble themselves with Writing; and, after acknowledging that he did with much Ingenuity, Constancy, Boldness, and greater Piety explode the Gods, tells us that many Heathens did for that reason not only decry those Books, and avoid reading them; but were also for solliciting the Senate to burn and abolish them: whereas, to use the judicious

---

[1] Quem quidem locum plene jamdudum homines pectoris vivi, tam Romanis Literis explicavere, quam Græcis, & ante omnes Tullius, Romani disertissimus Generis, nullam veritus Impietatis Invidiam, ingenue, constanter, & libere, quid super tali Opinatione sentiret, pietate cum majore monstravit. A quo si res sumere Judicii veritate conscriptas, non verborum Luculentias pergeretis, probata esset & hæc Causa, nec secundas (ut dicitur) actiones nobis ab Infantibus postularet. Sed quid aucupia verborum, splendoremque sermonis peti ab hoc dicam, cum sciam esse non paucos qui aversentur & fugiant Libros de hoc ejus, nec in aurem velint admittere Lectionem Opinionum suarum præsumpta vincentem? Cumque alios audiam mussitare indignanter & dicere, oportere statui per Senatum aboleantur ut hæc scripta, quibus Christiana Religio comprobetur, & vetustatis opprimatur auctoritas? Quinimo si fiditis exploratum vos dicere quicquam de Diis vestris, Erroris convincite Ciceronem; temeraria & impia dictitare refellitote, redarguite, comprobate: nam intercipere scripta, & publicatam velle submergere Lectionem, non est Deos defendere, sed veritatis Testificationem timere. *Lib.* 3. *adversus Gent.*

words

words of our Author, *to suppress those Books, or to prohibit the publick reading of them, was not to defend the Gods, but to fear the Testimony of Truth.* I cou'd name a great number of other Persons remarkable for their Valor, Piety, or Justice, who were much farther from being Idolaters than their Accusers; and shou'd no more be denominated Heathens, than those can be now call Mahometans, who, tho living at Mecca, disbelieve the Alcoran. Now, such as will have these to be Mahometans, or those to be Heathens, plainly show their Ignorance of what is meant by the Words, or that they perceive not the Distinction between the Law of Nature and all positive Institutions.

19. TO be short, MADAM, the Religion of the Gentiles (as contrary or superadded to the Light of Reason) is such as cou'd not influence Virtue or Morality very much in this Life, nor afford any certain Hopes or Security against the Terror of Death. 'Tis true, there were many among the Heathens, who, loath to believe their Religion so groundless and ridiculous as

Letter III. it ſeem'd to appear, eſpecially from the Deſcriptions of the Poets, wou'd have their numberleſs Gods to be nothing elſe but the various Appellations, Attributes, or Provinces of ſome one Being, whether it were the Sun, or BACCHUS, or any God beſides, of whom they had a better Opinion. Legiſlators did put the beſt face they cou'd upon the matter, and, without anxious Inquiry into the Truth or Falſhood of things, they approv'd of all that contributed to keep Mankind in order, that excited 'em to Virtue by Example and Rewards, that deter'd 'em from Vice by Puniſhments and Diſgrace. But others, as the well-meaning Philoſophers, allegoriz'd all their Doctrins into mere natural things, wherein the Deity manifeſts his Efficacy, Bounty, or Goodneſs; from which threefold Conſideration proceeded the famous Diſtinction of their Poetical, Political, and Philoſophical Theology. Yet the more diſcerning Perſons laught at theſe ſhifts, well knowing that it was impoſſible to make any tolerable Apology for moſt of their Fables. CICERO therefore condemns the Stoicks for pretending that all the Greek Theology was myſterious,

mysterious. *First* ZENO, [1] says he, *after him* CLEANTHES, *and then* CHRYSIPPUS, *were at great pains to no purpose, to give a reasonable Explication of commentitious Fables, and to account for the Etymology of the very Names of every God: which proceeding plainly shows that they believe not the Truth of these things in the literal sense.* However, to give a Specimen of their Allegorys, they made JUPITER and JUNO, to signify the Air and Clouds; NEPTUNE and THETIS, the Sea and Flouds; CERES and BACCHUS, the Earth and all its Productions; MERCURY and MINERVA, the ingenious Talents of the Mind, as Learning, Merchandize, Arts, or the like; CUPID and VENUS, our earnest Desires and amorous Inclinations; MARS and BELLONA, Dissensions and Wars; PLUTO and PROSERPINA,

[1] Magnam molestiam suscepit, ac minime necessariam, primus Zeno, post Cleanthes, deinde Chrysippus, commentitiarum fabularum reddere rationem: vocabulorum, cur quique ita appellati sint, causas explicare. Quod cum facitis, illud profecto confitemini, longe aliter rem se habere atque hominum opinio sit. *De Nat. Deor. l.* 3.

Mines,

Letter III.

Mines, Treasures, and whatever lies conceal'd under ground. So they proceeded to explain away the rest of the Gods; and, as Allegorys are as fruitful as our Imaginations, scarce any two Authors cou'd wholly agree in their Opinions. But supposing the Truth of the matter had bin as any or all of 'em wou'd have it, yet their Religion was not a whit the better, and deserv'd to be abolish'd; since, whatever were the Speculations of a few among the Learned, 'tis evident that the Vulgar took all these to be very real Gods, of whom they stood in mighty fear, and to whom they paid Divine Adoration: not to insist on the Trouble and Expensiveness of their Rites, or the Cheats and Dominion of the Priests. This was clearly perceiv'd by CICERO, who, enumerating the several kinds of the Heathen Gods, *From another Reason*, [1] says he, *and indeed a physical one, has proceeded a great multitude of Gods, which, being intro-*

---

[1] Alia quoque ex ratione, & quidem physica, magna fluxit multitudo Deorum, qui, inducti specie humana, fabulas Poetis suppeditaverunt, hominum autem vitam superstitione omni referserunt. *De Nat. Deor. l.* 2.

duc'd

possible to the higher Powers, and that these are Mysterys neither to be fathom'd or examin'd by the finite Understanding of Man; as may be read in almost all the Travels of all Nations.

21. HAVING given this summary Account, SERENA, of antient and modern Heathenism, we may remark that almost every Point of those superstitious and idolatrous Religions are in these or grosser Circumstances reviv'd by many Christians in our Western Parts of the Word, and by all the Oriental Sects: as Sacrifices, Incense, Lights, Images, Lustrations, Feasts, Musick, Altars, Pilgrimages, Fastings, religious Celibacy and Habits, Consecrations, Divinations, Sorcerys, Omens, Presages, Charms, the Worship of dead Men and Women, a continual Canonization of more, Mediators between God and Men, good and evil Dæmons, guardian Genius's, Male and Female tutelar Powers to whom they dedicate Temples, appoint Feasts and peculiar Modes of Worship, not only cantoning all Places among 'em, but likewise

Letter IV. It is not enough then to build on local Motion, which, as we said before, is but an Effect of this Action, as well as all the other Varietys in Nature; so is Rest, which is now generally acknowledg'd to be no Privation nor a State of absolute Inactivity, as much Force being necessary to keep Bodys at rest as to move them; wherefore local Motion and Rest are only relative Terms, perishable Modes, and no positive or real Beings.

10. 'TIS hard to determine what were the true Opinions of the most antient Sages of Greece; but the generality of Philosophers every where since ANAXAGORAS have laid down as a Principle, that Matter being of it self inactive, a dull and heavy Lump, the Divinity (which was acknowledg'd distinct from this Matter) communicated Motion to it, tho after a manner exceeding human Comprehension. Hence they proceed to show what Divisions this Motion made in Matter, what Particles of different Bulk and Figure thence were form'd, and how the Universe (I will not say how well) and all the Parts thereof came into their present

present State. SPINOSA, on the contrary, acknowledges no Being separate or different from the Substance of the Universe, no Being to give it Motion, to continue or to preserve it, if it has none of its own. He builds on all the common Notions about local Motion, without ever showing any Cause of it; being not willing to allow the Impulse of a presiding Deity, and unable (as you'll presently perceive) to produce a better, or as good a Reason. Yet he was of opinion that Matter was naturally inactive: for in the second part of his *Ethicks* or System, Proposition the thirteenth, Axiom the first, he says in express terms, [1] *All Bodys are either in motion or at rest*. And to let you see that he did not mean respective Rest, or the Resistance of other Bodys, in the Demonstration of the second Lemma he further affirms, that [2] *all Bodys may sometimes be absolutely mov'd, and sometimes be absolutely at rest*. There can be nothing more positive; yet if any or all

Letter IV.

---

[1] Omnia Corpora moventur vel quiescunt.

[2] Omnia Corpora —— absolute jam moveri, jam quiescere possunt.

the

Letter IV. the Parcels of Matter may be in absolute Rest, they must ever persist in that State without some external Cause to put 'em in motion, and this Cause he has no where assign'd; besides that all Matter may be inactive, if any part of it can ever be so.

11. SPINOSA has no where in his System attempted to define Motion or Rest, which is unpardonable in a Philosopher, whether done with or without design; and yet according to himself in his *Ethicks*, [1] *Motion and Rest are the Causes of all the Diversitys among Bodys*, thence [2] *proceeds the distinction of particular Bodys*, and [3] *an Infinity of things proceed from Motion and Rest.* In prosecuting this Subject I shall alledg nothing out of his other Books:

[1] Corpora ratione motus & quietis, celeritatis & tarditatis, & non ratione substantiæ ab invicem distinguuntur. *Lem.* 1. *ante Prop.* 14. *Part.* 2.

[2] Corpora res singulares sunt, quæ ratione motus & quietis ab invicem distinguuntur. *Demonstrat. Lem.* 3. *ante Prop.* 14. *Ibid.*

[3] Non tamen propterea Deus magis dici potest ex libertate voluntatis agere, quam propter ea quæ ex motu & quiete sequuntur (infinita enim ex his etiam sequuntur) dici potest ex libertate motus & quietis agere. *Corol.* 2. *Prop.* 3. *Part.* 1.

Books: becauſe that in his *Tractatus Theologico-Politicus* he has had no occaſion to treat of theſe matters; and that in one of his *Epiſtles* he declares himſelf not anſwerable for any thing in his *Demonſtration of* CARTESIUS's *Principles*; and this he oblig'd MEYER the Publiſher to tell the world in the Preface of the Book, which he has accordingly done: for he compos'd that Work at the requeſt of one of his Diſciples, and built his Demonſtrations on CARTESIUS's Definitions, Poſtulates, and Axioms, which are ſuppos'd but not believ'd to be true. So that the *Ethicks* (to which Title he has reduc'd all his Philoſophy) is his real Syſtem, wherein and in his *Letters* his genuine Sentiments of Philoſophy are only to be found. After dealing thus fairly with him (which is no more than Juſtice requires) there's no need of ſhowing by Inferences that he did not hold Motion to be an eternal Attribute of Matter; which if he had done, we cou'd not have believ'd it without good proof: I ſay, we are ſpar'd theſe pains, ſince he expreſly aſſerts the contrary, and he was ſurely beſt able to acquaint us with his own Opinion. In his firſt Letter

Letter IV.

Letter IV. to OLDENBURG, whereby he communicates to him some part of his *Ethicks*, thus he writes. *You must take heed that by Attribute I understand every thing that is conceiv'd by it self and in it self, in such a manner as that the Conception of it does not involve* or suppose *the Conception of any other thing: as Extension, for example, is conceiv'd by it self and in it self, but Motion not so; for it is conceiv'd to be in another thing, and the Conception of it involves Extension.* This is extremely plain and peremptory; nor shall we examine at present how true or false it may be of Extension, which is but an abstracted Idea, and no more conceivable without a Subject than Motion is.

12. SPINOSA then, who values himself in his *Ethicks* on deducing things from their first Causes (which the Schoolmen term *a priori*) SPINO-

---

* Ubi notandum me per attributum intelligere omne id quod concipitur per se & in se, adeo ut ipsius Conceptus non involvat Conceptum alterius rei: ut, ex. gr. Extensio per se & in se concipitur, at Motus non item; nam concipitur in alio, & ipsius Conceptus involvit Extensionem.

SA, I say, having given no account how Matter came to be mov'd or Motion comes to be continu'd, not allowing God as first Mover, neither proving nor supposing Motion to be an Attribute (but the contrary) nor indeed explaining what Motion is, he cou'd not possibly show how the Diversity of particular Bodys is reconcilable to the Unity of Substance, or to the Sameness of Matter in the whole Universe: wherefore I may safely conclude that his System is intirely precarious and without any sort of ground, indigested and unphilosophical. But lest your Affection shou'd biass you to think that such a great Man cou'd not stumble so at the Threshold, and that he has somewhere supply'd this enormous Defect tho it might escape my Observation, I hope you'll believe his own Words to a Person who wou'd not implicitly swear to his Philosophy, but whose Difference of Opinions did probably make as little Difference in their Affections as in yours and mine. 'Tis a very remarkable thing by what Delays, Shifts, and Excuses he wou'd avoid solving the Objections that were made to him on this Head, which

Letter IV.

Letter IV. keeps me ſtill in the Belief that he cou'd not bear to part with his Syſtem, nor to loſe the hopes of heading a new Sect.

13. BUT be this how it will (for we ought to be reſerv'd in divining the Thoughts or the Dead) the Author of the ſixty third Epiſtle in his *Poſthumous Works* preſſes him by a very ſenſible and modeſt Requeſt, which, without a good Anſwer, overthrows, as we have prov'd, the whole Fabrick of his Philoſophy. [1] *If you have leiſure,* ſays his Friend, *and that opportunity permits, I humbly beg of you the true Definition of Motion, as well as the Explication of that Definition: and after what manner (ſince Extenſion, as conſider'd in it ſelf, is indiviſible, immutable,* &c.) *we can ſhow* a priori *how ſuch and ſo many Varietys cou'd begin, and by conſequence the Exiſtence of Figures in the Particles of any Body, which yet*

[1] Si otium eſt & occaſio ſinit, a te ſubmiſſe peto veram Motus definitionem, ut & ejus explicationem; atque qua ratione (cum Extenſio, quatenus per ſe concipitur, indiviſibilis, immutabilis, &c. ſit) a priori deducere poſſimus tot tamque multas oriri poſſe varietates, & per conſequens Exiſtentiam figuræ in particulis

yet in every Body are various and different from the Figures of the Parts, which constitute the Form of another Body. Well; what says SPINOSA? or does he direct him to any place where this is already done to his hand? Far from it; for in the following Epistle he replies in these words: [1] *Now for the rest, that is to say, concerning Motion, and such things as relate to Method, because they are not yet written in Order, I keep 'em till another opportunity.* His Friend, who wou'd not be put off so slightly, and whose Thirst after Knowledg made him wait with Impatience, brings him again in mind of this Difficulty in the sixty ninth Epistle: [2] *I cannot without great difficulty conceive,* says he, *how a* priori *can be prov'd the Existence of Bodys which have Motions and Figures;* since

Letter IV.

culis alicujus Corporis, quæ tamen in quovis Corpore variæ & diversæ sunt a figuris partium quæ alterius Corporis formam constituunt.

[1] Cæterum, de reliquis, nimirum de Motu, quæque ad methodum spectant, quia nondum ordine conscripta sunt, in aliam occasionem reservo.

[2] Difficulter admodum concipere queo, quî a priori Corporum existentia demonstretur quæ Motus & Figuras habent; cum in extensione, rem absolute considerando, nîl tale occurrat.

Letter IV. *force in Extension, considering it by itself, nothing like these occurs.* To this SPINOSA answers without any Explication in the following Letter: [a] *It is not only difficult, as you say, but altogether impossible to demonstrate the Existence of particular Bodies from Extension, as* CARTESIUS *conceives it; that is to say, an inactive Bulk: for Matter that is at rest, will, as much as in it lies continue in its rest, nor can it be excited to Motion but by a more powerful external Cause; and for this reason I did not hesitate formerly to affirm that* CARTESIUS's *Principles of natural things were useless, I will not say absurd.* The other, who knew well enough that SPINOSA did not admit of any external Cause, tho his System (which was finish'd before) had not then appear'd, prays him with

[a] Ex Extensione, ut eam Cartesius concipit, molem scilicet quiescentem, corporum Existentiam demonstrare non tantum difficile, ut ais, sed omnino impossibile est: Materia enim quiescens, quantum in se est, in sua quiete perseverabit, nec ad motum concitabitur nisi a Causa potentiori externa; & hac de Causa non dubitavi olim affirmare rerum naturalium Principia Cartesiana inutilia esse, ne dicam absurda.

more

more earnestness than ever to speak his Thoughts without all disguize, for here he shelters himself under common Expressions. ' *I wish*, says his Friend in the one and seventieth Letter, *that you wou'd be pleas'd to gratify me in this particular, by telling me how the Variety of things can be shown to proceed from the Conception of Extension according to your Notions, since you mention'd* CARTESIUS'S *Opinion, in which he affirms to be able no other way to deduce this from Extension, but by supposing it to have bin produc'd therein from a Motion imprest by God.* CARTESIUS *therefore in my Judgment deduces the Existence of particular Bodys not from quiescent Matter, except the Supposition of God as Mover goes for nothing with you, since you have not your* Letter IV.

' Velim ut in hac re mihi gratificeris, indicando, qui ex conceptu Extensionis secundum tuas Meditationes varietas rerum a priori possit ostendi, quandoquidem meministi Opinionis Cartesianæ, in qua Cartesius statuit se eam ex Extensione nullo alio modo deducere posse, quam supponendo motu a Deo excitato hoc effectum fuisse in Extensione. Deducit ergo juxta meam Opinionem corporum Existentiam non ex quiescente materia, nisi forte suppositionem motoris Dei pro nihilo haberes, quandoquidem, qui illud ex

 essentia

Letter IV. *your self demonstrated how it shou'd necessarily follow from the Essence of God* a priori; *which,* CARTESIUS *going about to show, he believ'd it to exceed all human Comprehension. Wherefore I intreat this thing of you, well knowing you have other Thoughts, unless perhaps there be some culpable occasion that has hitherto kept you from making this Matter plain.* This Person has done Justice to CARTESIUS; for tho his System is at best but an ingenious Philosophical Romance, yet he was never so careless or inaccurate as to think of deducing the Variety and Difference of particular Bodys from mere Extension, and therefore suppos'd God at the beginning to have given a shake to the lazy Lump, from which his Matters of the first, second, and third Elements successively existed, and from these, after his manner, the Disposition of the whole Universe. But SPINOSA neither supposing the

essentia Dei a priori necessario sequi debeat, abs te non sit ostensum, id, quod Cartesius ostensurus, Captum humanum superare credebat. Quare a te hanc rem requiro, sciens bene te alias Cogitationes habere, nisi alia sontica subsit forte causa, quare illud hactenus manifestum facere nolueris, &c,

same

ſame Principle, nor eſtabliſhing any Letter other to explain the Varietys of par- IV. ticular Bodys in the Identity of Subſtance, you'll own, I doubt not, that without any Artifice, Paſſion, or Intereſt, I have clearly prov'd what I undertook to you, that his Philoſophy is built on no certain or probable Foundation, but on gratuitous Suppoſitions, from which he deduces what he and his Followers call Demonſtrations. He was accuſtom'd to this way of pretending to demonſtrate things in a Geometrical Method, tho he knew 'em to be falſe, ſince thus he had before demonſtrated CARTESIUS's Principles. But that very Work is a memorable Example how eaſily People may be deceiv'd by this Method (tho in it ſelf abſolutely certain) if they are not us'd to make long Deductions without miſſing one Link in the Chain, if they take any thing for ſelf evident which needs it ſelf to be prov'd, or any thing for prov'd from the Authority of others or their own Prepoſſeſſions. But to return to his Friend, all the Anſwer he receiv'd to his laſt Intreaty was in general words; for in the two and ſeventieth Epiſtle, SPINOSA after rejecting

Letter IV. jecting CARTESIUS's Definition of Matter, thus bespeaks him: * *What you desire of me, whether the Variety of things can be demonstrated,* a priori *from the mere Conception of Extension, I think I have already shown this to be impossible, and that consequently Matter was ill defin'd by* CARTESIUS *from Extension; whereas it ought to be necessarily explain'd by some Attribute, which expresses an eternal and infinite Essence. But, if I live, perhaps I may some other time deal more plainly with you about these matters: for I have not bin able hitherto to dispose any thing in order about them.* We do not find that he ever did so about Motion, which makes it the more inexcusable, because, altho his *Ethicks* were compleated at this time, yet he might change, add, or take away what he wou'd,

* Quod petis, an ex solo Extensionis conceptu rerum varietas a priori possit demonstrari, credo me jam satis clare ostendisse id impossibile esse, ideoque materiam a Cartesio male definiri per Extensionem; sed eam necessario debere explicari per Attributum, quod aeternam, & infinitam Essentiam exprimat. Sed de his forsan aliquando, si vita suppetit, clarius tecum agam; nam huc usque nihil de his ordine disponere mihi licuit.

since

since the Book was not publish'd till after his Death. Neither could Motion be the Attribute he means here, having directly declar'd the contrary before, and nothing appearing to favor this Notion in all his Works. Letter IV.

14. I NEED not require a better proof that Men of the greatest Candor and Judgment may be in many things seduc'd by Prejudice, since you never perceiv'd this Flaw, my Friend; and that you ever extoll'd SPINOSA, for demonstrating all things *a priori*. On the contrary, in your Letter to me of the Tenth Instant, you much insist on the Difficultys which accompany the common Systems of Motion, taking it, I suppose, for granted that your Hero had mended the matter, which you see he never did. To take my leave of him therefore, and to apply my Discourse to your self, it is notorious that most of those Difficultys you mention, proceed from Peoples confounding the Cause with the Effect, or the moving Force with local Motion; and when they think they have given its true Definition, they have really said nothing but that Motion

Letter IV. tion is Motion, only diversifying their Terms a little; for when a Bowl runs on the Green, and the Definition of Motion is ask'd, 'tis gravely answer'd, that *it is the removing of one Body from the Neighborhood of others*, &c. and this the Bowlers know as well as the Philosopher, seeing it daily with their own Eyes; but 'tis the Cause of this Effect they desire to hear explain'd, of which he's ordinarily as ignorant as they.

15. YOU say very truly that even those who carefully distinguish the Cause and the Effect, are yet extremely puzzl'd about the *moving Force* it self, what sort of Being it is; where it resides, in Matter or without it; by what means it can move Matter; how it passes from one Body to another; or is divided between many Bodys while others are at rest, and a thousand more such Riddles. Wherefore not being able to discover any such real Being in Nature, nor to determin whether it be a Body or Spirit, and yet less to make it a Mode, since (among other Objections) no Accident can pass from one Subject to

to another, nor be without its particular Cause in any Subject whatsoever, and that it may be intirely destroy'd the Subject remaining safe, they are forc'd at last to have recourse to God, and to maintain that as he communicated Motion to Matter at the beginning, so he still begets and continues it whenever, and as long as there's occasion for it, and that he actually concurs to every Motion in the Universe. But this System is subject to more fatal Consequences than those they wou'd avoid by it: for besides that they hereby destroy what many have said about God's impressing Motion on Matter at the beginning, as something that was of it self sufficient for the future; they farther make God the Author of all the Wickedness in Nature, tho Motion were still but a Mode. 'Tis he, for example, that actually moves the Tongue of a lying Witness, the Hand and Dagger of a Murderer, with such other palpable Difficultys, which all their moral and physical Distinctions are not able to solve. But why shou'd I throw away any Words on this System, since in all times, as CICERO observes, when the Philosophers

Letter IV. sophers are ignorant of the Cause of any thing, they presently betake themselves for refuge and sanctuary to * God, which is not to explain things, but to cover their own Negligence or Shortsightedness, their Vanity not suffering them to allow any other Cause, but God's immediate Concourse to what they are not able to unfold.

16. YOU do not foresee perhaps what Doubts you create to your self, and what Work you cut out for me, in demanding my particular Opinion about Motion. 'Tis easier at any time to find out the Defects of others than to supply them, and a Man is very like to be wrong understood who delivers his Opinion (especially if altogether new) before it be guarded with its Proofs and Explication: but our Friendship not allowing me to deny you any thing in my power, I shall be open and free with you in this particular. I hold then that *Mo-*

* Sed omnium talium rerum ratio reddenda est: quod vos, cum facere non potestis, tanquam in aram confugitis ad Deum. *De Nat. Deor. l.* 3.

tion

tion is essential to Matter, that is to say, as inseparable from its Nature as Impenetrability or Extension, and that it ought to make a part of its Definition. But as in Matter we distinguish the *Quantity* of particular Bodys and the *Extension* of the whole, of which these Quantitys are but several Determinations or Modes, existing and perishing by their several Causes: so, the better to be understood, I wou'd have this Motion of the Whole be call'd *Action*, and all local Motions, as direct or circular, fast or slow, simple or compounded, be still call'd *Motion*, being only the several changeable *Determinations* of the *Action* which is always in the Whole, and in every Part of the same, and without which it cou'd not receive any Modifications. I deny that Matter is or ever was an inactive dead Lump in absolute Repose, a lazy and unweildy thing; and when I write expresly on this Subject to you, I hope to evince that this Notion alone accounts for the same Quantity of Motion in the Universe, that it alone proves there neither needs nor can be any Void, that Matter cannot be truly defin'd without it, that

Letter IV.

Letter IV. that it solves all the Difficultys about the moving Force, and all the rest which we have mention'd before.

17. BUT you'l say that, besides the Singularity of the Opinion, I shall make a world of Adversarys by reason of the many Hypotheses and Doctrins which it unavoidably destroys. To this I answer, that the Offence is taken, but not given; and that I shall thereby be nothing disquieted, provided I be able to contribute any thing towards the Discovery of Truth. This is not a System of Accommodation, such as those which some invent to reconcile other different Systems, tho they are not certain that their own is more true than the rest. But if I be able to prove from the nature of the thing it self, and not to favor or oppose any Cause, that *Action is essential to Matter*, that Matter cannot be rightly conceiv'd nor consequently be rightly defin'd without it, that nothing can be accounted for in Matter without this essential Action, and that it is easily shown to exist in the most heavy or hard Bodys; then they may quarrel (who have a mind to it) with

God

God or Nature, and not with me, who am but their humble Interpreter. After all, I apprehend no Enemys if I shou'd ever publish to the World what I may write to any Friend on this Subject; for every Party is necessitated to explain the Phenomena of Nature by Motion: and therefore such as believe Matter created, may as well conceive that God at the beginning endu'd it with Action as well as with Extension; and those who believe it eternal, may as well believe it eternally active, as eternally divisible; nor can they ever account for any Change in Nature without admitting this, as I have prov'd before against SPINOSA. My only business is to prove *Matter necessarily active as well as extended*, and thence to explain as much as I can of its Affections; but not to meddle in the Disputes which others may raise about its Original or Duration.

18. YOU may perceive, SIR, that I have a great deal of leisure, and nothing to make me uneasy, or at least that I won't be made so, when I can take occasion to write so long a Letter from a few hints in a couple of yours. But it

Letter IV. is impossible not to acquire a more dilated Understanding by your Correspondence. After so much Philosophy about the Primitive World, I shall trouble you with nothing that passes in the present; and I desire this particular favor of you, that in the Letters with which you'l please to honor me during my Stay in this Solitude (which I hope will be very many) you wou'd not mention a word of News: for there's something in all such Occurrences, which engages us to interest our selves more than in many Peoples Opinion we are concern'd to do; and yet, according as it goes with publick Affairs, I cannot for my Life refrain from rejoicing, or being angry, or growing sad like others, which perhaps proceeds from very good Reasons, but with which I wou'd not willingly be disquieted here. Still I except from the foregoing Instructions all that regards your Family or our other Friends, in whose Welfare, and particularly in your own, none can receive more real Satisfaction, than, SIR, your most humble and affectionate Servant.

LETTER

LETTER V.

Motion essential to Matter; *in Answer to some Remarks by a noble Friend on the* Confutation of SPINOSA.

Nunc quæ mobilitas sit reddita Materiai
Corporibus, paucis licet hinc cognoscere, Memmi. Lucret. l. 2.

1. PARDON me, SIR, if I doubt whether the favorable Character you are pleas'd to bestow on *the Confutation of* SPINOSA, proceeds from your Kindness

Letter V. or your Judgment. But what makes me flatter my self that you wrote your genuine Thoughts about the first part ~~of that Letter to our worthy Friend,~~ is your making some Objections against the latter part, wherein I have barely declar'd my Opinion, that *Matter is necessarily active as well as extended.* To this you cannot easily agree, and neither he nor I can blame you for it, unless at the same time we wou'd rashly condemn our selves when we were of your mind. But as our Opinion ought to go for nothing without good Reasons, so we admit of no Right from Possession, of no Privilege by Prescription in Philosophy, how much soever we allow it in national Laws or Customs. Authority is to decide matters of Fact, but not to determine the Truths of Nature. You ventur'd fair, I must acknowledg, to make your Observations and Objections before I gave any notice or hint of my Arguments: but this very Proceeding declares how untenable you believe my Assertion to be, even so unguarded and absurd, that any Person cou'd easily guess at the little that might be plausibly offer'd for such a Paradox.

This is but a natural Construction of your meaning, and such Thoughts as People are extremely apt to entertain of any Notion that contradicts the common Belief, especially if such a Belief has continu'd very long in possession, and has bin very universally receiv'd. In the Answer you desire of me, I shall follow the Thread of your own Letter; and take care to be as brief, as the indispensable Law of Perspicuity will permit. Letter V.

2. YOU take my Meaning very right in urging, that *if Activity ought to enter into the Definition of Matter, it ought likewise to express the Essence thereof*: for certainly all the Propertys of any thing shou'd follow or be knowable from its Definition; else the Definition is not distinguishing and adequate, but confuse and imperfect. In my Opinion therefore Matter has bin hitherto but half, or rather a third part defin'd by Extension, from which alone many of its Modifications can follow by no means; and this is the reason, why none of the motive Effects have bin consider'd as essential to it, but adventitious and of a different sort, because

 not

Letter V. not contain'd in any of the Terms of its Definition: whereas Matter being defin'd active as well as extended (to which you may add Solidity, with the incomparable Mr. LOCK) then all the motive Effects follow very naturally, and need not be explain'd by any other Cause, no more than the Consequences of Extension. Supposing it an Error that Motion is extraneous to Matter, you'll own that the ordinary Definitions which are built upon this Supposition, have greatly contributed to settle it firmly in the Minds of men; they being thus accustom'd to deprive Matter of Motion in their Speech and Writing from the beginning, which kept 'em for ever after from revoking it in doubt, but rather making it a self-evident Principle: and you know that such as had designs of gaining Reputation by introducing false Doctrins that favor'd their Designs, or of maintaining their Authority in supporting absurd Persuasions already establish'd, did make it a standing Rule that *Principles must not be disputed*; and then they canoniz'd for Principles, whatever Maxims they found most conducible to their purpose. But if Motion be essen-

tial

tial to Matter, it must be likewise as essential to its Definition. Letter V.

3. I OWN what you next object, that *before such a Definition is made, the necessary Activity of Matter ought to be clearly prov'd*, which to do, in the Sequel of this Letter, is my Intention; and to endeavor the recommending of this Definition by the Reasons I shall produce to show that all the Matter in Nature, every Part and Parcel of it, has bin ever in motion, and can never be otherwise; that the Particles which lie in the midst of the most solid and bulky Rocks, in the heart of Iron Bars or Gold Ingots, are as well in constant Action, as those of Fire, or Air, or Water, tho not according to the same Determinations, nor in the same Degrees, no more than these last mention'd, compar'd among themselves: for this Action is equally natural and internal to them all, and to all other Classes of Matter in the Universe; tho their specifick Motions be so various and different, which proceeds from their several ways of affecting one another. But it's time enough to think of a new Definition, when this essen-

Letter V. tial Motion is evidently prov'd.

4. YOU once thought it inconceivable, it seems, I should ever maintain that *Matter cannot as much as be conceiv'd without an Action of its own, or under some Effect of such an Action*; and I still maintain, that Matter can no more be conceiv'd without Motion than without Extension, and that the one is as inseparable from it as the other. Your conceiving Faculty I know to be much more delicate than mine, wherefore I wou'd have you try it a little on this Subject, and then to make me comprehend what Idea you have fram'd of Matter without Action. It must be something depriv'd of all Figure or Color, neither heavy nor light, rough or smooth, sweet or sour, hot or cold, void (in a word) of all sensible Qualitys, without Parts, Proportion, or any Relation whatsoever: since all these depend immediately on Motion, as well as the Forms of all corporeal Beings, their Generation, Succession, and Corruption, by the numberless Mixtures, Transpositions, and other Arrangements of their Parts, all which are the natural and undoubted

Letter V.

Effects of Motion, or rather Motion it self under these several Names and Determinations. The commonly acknowledg'd Divisibility of Matter is also an undeniable Argument that it cannot be conceiv'd without Motion, since it is Motion that diversifies or divides it; which is therefore presuppos'd as well as Extension in the Idea of Divisibility, and consequently the one is as essential to Matter as the other. How can you conceive that Matter is any thing or a Substance, unless it be endu'd with Action? How can it be the Subject of Accidents (according to the vulgar Definition) since all Accidents are nothing else but the several Determinations of Action in Matter, diversify'd as they are differently plac'd with relation to our Senses; but in reality not distinct from our Imagination, or from the thing it self wherein they are said to exist? Roundness is nothing different from the round Body (which is as true of all Figures) for this Roundness is not the Name of any real thing, but only a word to express the particular manner of a certain Body. Neither are Hot or Cold, Sounds, Smells, or Colors, so much as even the

Man-

Letter V.

Manners or Postures of the things themselves, but the Names we give to their ways of affecting our Imagination; for most things are conceiv'd by us with respect to our own Bodys, and not to their true Nature: wherefore what is sweet to one is sour to another, what is rough to me is smooth to you, what is pleasure to the Healthy is pain to the Sick; tho most mens Organs being fram'd very like one another, they are consequently affected much after the same manner, yet still with some degrees of Difference. But these, and all other Differences in Matter proceeding from several Changes, or these very things being but the Conceptions of different Motions, I think I may warrantably affirm that Matter is never conceiv'd but under some Notion of Action, which before I end I design to show to be as true of Rest it self. Now strip me Matter of Motion (if you can) and I undertake before-hand to divine your Conception of it, which must be the very same with those who try'd such Projects before you: for their *Materia prima* was *quæ neque est quid, neque est quale, neque est quantum, neque quicquam eorum quibus Ens denominatur*;

natur; which is in a great many words to say, that it is nothing at all. Letter V.

5. BUT you affirm that *the Extension of Matter is very easily known, if not self-evident, but not its Activity*; wherein I must beg leave to dissent from you, asserting that the one is no less easy to be known than the other, and neither of 'em doubted or mistaken, but by such as judg of things from Appearances, Custom, or Authority, without consulting their own Reason, arguing in which Method they may as well prove the Moon to be no bigger than a large Cheshire Cheese: for as the Vulgar believe that there is no Extension, where they perceive no visible Object; so those, who wou'd take it ill to be rankt in other things with the Vulgar, yet agree with them in this, thinking that there's no Action, where they can see no local or determinate Motion. Experience shows that great numbers of Adversarys are no Argument against the Truth of any thing whatsoever. The plainest things in the World have bin mighty Secrets for whole Ages; and we know that it's hard to find a thing, where no body

Letter V. dreams of looking for it. Have a little patience, SIR, and I may be so happy as to be capable of showing you what led all Sects of Philosophers as well as the Vulgar, to believe the Sluggishness of Matter, tho divers of the former were aware of its actual universal Motion, which from the Prejudice of their Infancy, they were ready to ascribe to any Cause rather than to the right one; and this has very often oblig'd 'em to feign very ill-sorted and ridiculous Hypotheses.

6. I APPROVE of your fourth Observation (for you know I wou'd not easily disagree with you in any thing) that *many of the most learned Philosophers contend for a Vacuum, which Notion seems to be grounded on the Deadness or Inactivity of Matter*: to which I add, that some of those Philosophers deny (with the Epicureans) the Void to have any substantial Extension, and will have it to be nothing; while the rest make it an extended Substance, which is neither Body nor Spirit. These Notions have rais'd a world of Disputes about the nature of Space. The Opinion of a Void is one of the numberless erroneous Consequences

quences of defining Matter only by Extension, of making it naturally inactive, and of thinking it divided into real Parts every way independent of one another. On these Suppositions it is impossible there shou'd not be a Void; but 'tis as impossible that ten thousand Absurditys shou'd not follow from thence. What we call Parts in Matter, may be prov'd to be but the different Conceptions of its Affections, the distinctions of its Modifications; which Parts are therefore only imaginary or relative, but not real and absolutely divided: for Water, as such, can be generated, divided, and corrupted, increas'd and diminish'd; but not when consider'd as Matter.

7. ON this occasion, to avoid all Ambiguity, 'tis convenient to inform you, that by Bodys I understand certain Modifications of Matter, conceiv'd by the Mind as so many limited Systems, or particular Quantitys mentally abstracted, but not actually separated from the Extension of the Universe. We therefore say that one Body is bigger or less than another, is broken or dissolv'd, from the multifarious Change of Modifications:

Letter V.

fications: but we cannot properly ſay that Matters are bigger one than another, becauſe there's but one ſort of Matter in the Univerſe; and if it be infinitely extended, it can have no abſolute Parts independent of one another, Parts and Particles being conceiv'd as I told you juſt now that Bodys were. A world of other words are invented to help our Imagination, like Scaffolds for the Convenience of the Workmen; but which muſt be laid aſide when the Building is finiſh'd, and not be miſtaken for the Pillars or Foundation. Of this ſort are Great and Small, for example, which are but mere Compariſons of the Mind, and not the Names of any poſitive Subjects; as you are Big in reſpect of your little Siſter, but Little in reſpect of an Elephant, and ſhe is Big when compar'd to her Parrot, but very Little when ſhe ſtands by her Mother. Theſe and ſuch words are very ſerviceable when rightly apply'd; yet they are often abus'd, and from relative or modal, are made real, abſolute, and poſitive: ſuch are Bodys, Parts, Particles, Somthing, a certain Being, and the like, which may be well allow'd in the Practice of Life, but never in the Specu-

Speculations of Philosophy.

8. BUT to return to your Objection; others who admitted no real, but only modal and respective Parts in Nature, yet cou'd never with all their Subtilty bring any Arguments against a Void, but what their Adversarys cou'd easily ruin, because they agreed with them in making Matter inactive. You, that understand so well the History of Philosophy, know that the Difficultys appear to be equal on both sides, which has induc'd many to believe that the thing is in its own nature inexplicable, throwing the fault (as they often unjustly do) on their own Conceptions, which they find unsatisfy'd; and not on the precarious Suppositions of both Partys, which they do not perceive. There is nothing more certain than that of two Contradictorys the one must be always true, as the other must be always false; and tho it be therefore indisputable that either there is a Void, or that all is full (to use their improper Expression) tho it be plain that the Truth is within the narrow Compass of these two short Propositions, yet neither side has bin hitherto

Letter V. therto able to demonstrate which of 'em is the true Opinion, because they have both argu'd from a false Medium, from which nothing but Falsitys and Absurditys cou'd naturally follow.

9. BUT if you are once persuaded, SIR, as I hope you quickly will, that Matter is active as well as extended, all your difficultys about a *Vacuum* must fall to the ground. For as those particular or limited Quantitys, which we call such or such Bodys, are but several Modifications of the general Extension of Matter in which they are all contain'd, and which they neither increase nor diminish: so (as an adequate Parallel) all the particular or local Motions of Matter are but the several Determinations of its general Action, directing it this or that way, by these or those Causes, in this or that manner, without giving it any Augmentation or Diminution. Indeed in all Treatises of the ordinary Laws of Motion, you meet with the several degrees of Motion that any Body loses or acquires; but those Laws concern the Quantity of the Action of particular Bodys on

one another, and not the Action of Matter in general; as particular Quantitys of Matter are measur'd by other lesser Quantitys, but not the Extension of the Whole. The Mathematicians compute the Quantitys and Proportions of Motion, as they observe Bodys to act on one another, without troubling themselves about the physical Reasons of what every person allows, being a thing which does not always concern them, and which they leave the Philosophers to explain: tho the latter wou'd succeed better in their Reasons, if they did more acquaint themselves before-hand with the Observations and Facts of the former, as Mr. NEWTON justly [1] observes.

10. THERE is no inseparable Attribute of Matter, but has number-

---

[1] In Mathesi investigandæ sunt virium Quantitates & Rationes illæ, quæ ex conditionibus quibuscunque positis consequentur: denique ubi in physicam descenditur, conferendæ sunt hæ Rationes cum Phænomenis, ut innotescat quænam virium Conditiones singulis Corporum attractivorum generibus competant; & tum demum de virium Speciebus, Causis, & Rationibus Physicis tutius disputare licebit. *Philos. Nat. Princip. Math.* p. 192.

Letter V. less Modifications proper to it self as well as Extension. So has Solidity, so has Action; and yet all the Attributes must concur in producing the peculiar Modes of each, because they are still but the Consideration of the self-same Matter under different respects. To say then, as you do after a Croud of Philosophers, that *if there be no Void, there is consequently no place for* C *to remove into, nor any Elbow-room for* B *to push* C; for you, I repeat it, to speak in this manner, is not only to have the same gross Conception of Space with your Farmers, but also to suppose the Points *B* and *C*, and all or most of the Points about them, to be really fixt, and in absolute Repose. But you shou'd not run with a multitude to commit Mistakes, no more than to do evil; and if I succeed in proving the natural, essential, intrinsick, and necessary Action of Matter, then you may easily perceive that these Objections will be no longer Difficultys, and that all your Circles of contiguous Balls, your Fish on the point of moving in the Water, and the rest of those thredbare Examples must be employ'd on some other occasions; because all these

suppose

supose an absolute Rest, as well as the Generation of Motion, which is the thing in question; and cou'd it be prov'd, there wou'd be no solid answering of such Arguments for a *Vacuum*. Letter V.

11. I HINTED something to you before about the abuse of Words in Philosophy, and we may instance particularly certain Terms invented to very good purpose by Mathematicians; but misunderstood or perverted by others, and not seldom very wrongly apply'd by certain Mathematicians themselves, which can never fail to happen when abstracted Notions are taken for real Beings, and then laid down as Principles whereon to build Hypotheses. Thus the Mathematical Lines, Surfaces, and Points have bin maintain'd to exist in reality, and many Conclusions thence deduc'd, tho very unhappily; as that Extension was compounded of Points, which is to say, that Length, Breadth, and Thickness are form'd of what is neither long, nor broad, nor thick, or Measure of no Quantity. So the word *Infinite* has bin wonderfully perplex'd;

Letter V. which has given occasion to a thousand Equivocations and Errors. Number was made infinite; as if it follow'd, because Units may be added to one another without end, that there actually existed an infinite Number. Of this nature are, infinite Time, the infinite Cogitation of Man, asymptot Lines, and a great many other boundless Progressions, which are infinite only with respect to the Operations of our Minds, but not so in themselves: for whatever is really infinite, does actually exist as such; whereas what only may be infinite, is very positively not so.

12. BUT no Word has bin more misapply'd, nor consequently has given occasion to more Disputes than Space, which is only an abstracted Notion (as you shall perceive hereafter) or the Relation that any thing has to other Beings at a distance from it, without any Consideration of what lies between them, tho they have at the same time a real Existence. Thus Place is either the relative Position of a thing with respect to the circumambient Bodys, or the Room it fills with its own Bulk, and from which it is conceiv'd to exclude

Letter V.

clude all other Bodys, which are but mere Abstractions, the Capacity nothing differing from the Body contain'd: and so Distance is the Measure between any two Bodys, without regard to the things whose Extension is so measur'd. Yet because the Mathematicians had occasion to suppose Space without Matter, as they did Duration without Things, Points without Quantity, and the like; the Philosophers, who cou'd not otherwise account for the Generation of Motion in Matter which they held to be inactive, imagin'd a real Space distinct from Matter, which they held to be extended, incorporeal, immovable, homogeneal, indivisible, and infinite. But this whole Dispute depends on the Action and Infinity of Matter. In the first place, if Matter it self be essentially active, there's no need to help it to Motion by this Invention, nor is there any Generation of Motion. Secondly, if it be infinite, it can have no separate Parts that move independently of one another in crooked or streight Lines, notwithstanding those Modifications which we call particular divisible Bodys. Thirdly, Matter must be like-

Letter V.

wise homogeneal, if it has Action of it self as well as Solidity or Extension, without being divided into Parts. And fourthly, if it be infinite, the Universe must be without all local Motion, there being no fix'd Points without it, to which it might be successively apply'd, nor any place into which it cou'd possibly remove.

13. PROCEEDING, SIR, according to the Order of your Remarks, I shall briefly endeavor to prove these several Points. I am not insensible that I oppose a Notion universally receiv'd, and that in this particular Article of Space I am said to have the greatest Man in the world against me, who yet cannot grow any thing less, tho he shou'd happen herein to be mistaken; since the Demonstrations and Discoverys of his unparallel'd Book remain intirely true without it. For my part, I can no more believe an absolute Space distinct from Matter, as the place of it; than that there is an absolute Time, different from the things whose Duration are consider'd. And yet Mr. NEWTON is thought not only to believe these things, but also to put them

them both on the same foot. *Times and Spaces*, says [1] he, *are as it were their own Places, and those of all other things. All the things in the Universe are in Time as to the Order of Succession, and in Space as to the Order of Situation. 'Tis essential to 'em that they be Places; and to think these primary Places can be mov'd, is absurd. These are therefore absolute Places, and the Translations from them are the only absolute Motions.* I am convinc'd that these Words are capable of receiving an Interpretation favorable to my Opinion; but I chuse to cite them in the sense wherein they are commonly understood: besides that his Book (as I said before) is neither way concern'd.

Letter V.

14. AS for your alledging (to infer the Inactivity of Matter, as well as a *Vacuum*) that *one Body is heavier or lighter than another of equal Bulk*; you

[1] Tempora & Spatia sunt sui-ipsorum & rerum omnium quasi loca. In Tempore, quoad ordinem Successionis, in Spatio, quoad ordinem Situs, locantur universa. De illorum essentia est ut sint loca, & loca primaria moveri absurdum est. Hæc sunt igitur absoluta loca, & solæ Translationes de his locis sunt absoluti Motus. *P.* 7.

Letter V. must suppose that Levity and Gravity are not mere Relations, the Comparisons of certain Situations and external Pressures; but that they are real Beings, or absolute and inherent Qualitys, which is now by every body exploded, and contrary to all that you know your self of Mechanicks. It may not be difficult to persuade even Persons of a moderate Capacity, that there cou'd be no Levity or Gravity in the suppos'd Chaos, and that these Qualitys wholly depend on the Constitution and Fabrick of the Universe; which is to say, that they are the Consequences of the World in actual Being, and the necessary Effects of its present Order, but not essential Attributes of Matter, the same Body becoming heavy or light by turns, according as it is plac'd among other Bodys, and there being nothing better known, than that many things are not sometimes in a state of Levity or Gravity. To imagine that any Parcel of Matter has Levity or Gravity of it self, because you see those Effects in the Fabrick of the World; or to deduce it from the common Laws of Gravitation, is not only to imagine Matter alike

alike affected in all Places, but that the Wheels, and Springs, and Chains of a Watch, can perform all those Motions separately which they do together. And yet it was from such false Suppositions, that the Philosophers, in their several Formations of the World, invented the Fable of the four Elements; orderly placing themselves according to their different degrees of Gravity and Levity; the Earth undermost or in the Center, next to that the Water, then the Seat of the Air, and uppermost of all the Fire. All Sorts and Sects of People have bin superstitiously fond of this primary Chaos, a Notion as confus'd and monstrous as the Import of the Name, and built in every step on Suppositions that are not only arbitrary, but utterly false and chimerical: such is the gross Conception of the Number and Unmixedness of the four Elements, drawn from the most compounded Bodys in the world; such is the Levity and Gravity of the dancing Particles; and such the Separation of the Seeds of things (as they speak) which without such Levity and Gravity cou'd not be perform'd, nor indeed on these very Conditions, without

Letter V. without an Almighty Architect, which they did not always take care to provide; or furnish'd him with such wretched Tools and Contrivance, as show'd the Meanness of their own Understanding, the sole Model by which they form'd him. Such a precarious Supposition (in a word) is Matter's having bin at any time in this Confusion, without ascertaining how long or for what reason, with a thousand more the like Absurditys, which every man may easily represent to himself from these few Instances. This may also serve for an Example, how little stress is to be laid on universal Consent, or rather on any epidemical and common Error that makes pretences to that Name.

15. BUT not to ramble into Digressions, tho never so natural, you own that *most Bodys are in actual Motion, which can be no Argument that they have bin always so, or that there are not others in absolute Repose.* I grant that such a Consequence does not necessarily follow, tho the thing in it self be true. But however, it may not be amiss to consider, how far this

actual Motion reaches and is allow'd, before we come to treat of Rest. Tho the Matter of the Universe be every where the same, yet, according to its various Modifications, it is conceiv'd to be divided into numberless particular Systems, Vortexes, or Whirlpools of Matter; and these again are subdivided into other Systems greater or less, which depend on one another, as every one on the Whole, in their Centers, Texture, Frame, and Coherence. Our Sun (for example) is the Center of one of those bigger Systems, which contains a great many lesser ones within the Sphere of its Activity, as all the Planets that move about it: and these are subdivided into yet lesser Systems that depend on them, as his Satellites wait upon Jupiter, and the Moon on the Earth; the Earth again is divided into the Atmosphere, Ground, Water, and other principal Parts; these again into Men, Birds, Beasts, Trees, Plants, Fishes, Worms, Insects, Stones, Metals, and a thousand other differences. Now as all these depend in a Link on one another, so their Matter (to speak in the usual Language) is mutually resolv'd into each other: for Earth,

Earth, and Water, and Air, and Fire, are not only closely blended and united, but likewise interchangeably transform'd in a perpetual Revolution; Earth becoming Water, Water Air, Air Æther, and so back again in Mixtures without End or Number. The Animals we destroy contribute to preserve us, till we are destroy'd to preserve other things, and become Grass, or Plants, or Water, or Air, or something else that helps to make other Animals, and they one another, or other Men; and these again turn into Stone, or Wood, or Mettals, or Minerals, or Animals again, or become Parts of all these and of a great many other Things, Animals and Vegetables daily consuming and devouring each other; so true it is that every thing lives by the Destruction of another. All the Parts of the Universe are in this constant Motion of destroying and begetting, of begetting and destroying: and the greater Systems are acknowledg'd to have their ceasless Movements as well as the smallest Particles, the very central Globes of the Vortexes turning about their own Axis; and every Particle in the Vortex gravitating towards the Center. Our Bodys, however we may flatter our selves,

ſelves, differ nothing from thoſe of other Creatures, but like them receive Increaſe or Diminution by Nutrition and Evacuation, by Accretion, Tranſpiration, and ſeveral other ways, giving ſome Parts of ours to other Bodys, and receiving again of theirs, not altogether the ſame yeſterday as to day, nor to continue the ſame to morrow, being alive in a perpetual Flux like a River, and in the total Diſſolution of our Syſtem at death to become Parts of a thouſand other things at once; our Carcaſes partly mixing with the Duſt and Water of the Earth, partly exhal'd and evaporated into the Air, flying to ſo many different places, mixing and incorporating with innumerable things.

16. NO Parts of Matter are ty'd to any one Figure or Form, loſing and changing their Figures and Forms continually, that is, being in perpetual Motion, clipt, or worn, or ground to pieces, or diſſolv'd by other Parts, acquiring their Figures, and theſe theirs, and ſo on inceſſantly; Earth, Air, Fire, and Water, Iron, Wood, and Marble, Plants and Animals, being rarefy'd or condens'd,

Letter V. condens'd, or liquify'd or congeal'd, or dissolv'd or coagulated, or any other way resolv'd into one another. The whole Face of the Earth exhibits those Mutations every minute to our Eyes, nothing continuing one hour numerically the same; and these Changes being but several kinds of Motion, are therefore the incontestable Effects of some universal Action. But the Changes in the Parts make no Change in the Universe: for it is manifest that the continual Alterations, Successions, Revolutions, and Transmutations of Matter, cause no Accession or Diminution therein, no more than any Letter is added or lost in the Alphabet by the endless Combinations and Transpositions thereof into so many different Words and Languages: for a thing no sooner quits one Form than it puts on another, leaving as it were the Theater in a certain dress, and appearing again in a new one, which produces a perpetual Youthfulness and Vigor, without any Decay or Decrepitness of the World, as some have foolishly imagin'd, contrary not only to Reason, but to Experience; the World, with all the Parts and Kinds thereof, con-

continuing

tinuing at all times in the same condition. The great Systems of the Universe being subdivided into gradual and lesser Systems of Matter, the Individuals of the latter do perish indeed, tho they are not annihilated, continuing only a certain time in their particular Forms, according to the Strength or Weakness of their Disposition, Structure, or Constitution, which we call the natural age or time of such a thing; yet if this Constitution, before its ordinary Period, be destroy'd by more prevalent circumambient Motions, in such cases we commonly call it Violence or Accident, as that a murder'd young man is dead before his time. But the Species still continues by Propagation, notwithstanding the Decay of the Individuals; and the Death of our Bodys, is but Matter going to be drest in some new Form: the Impressions may vary, but the Wax continues still the same, and indeed Death is in effect the very same thing with our Birth; for as to die is only to cease to be what we formerly were, so to be born is to begin to be somthing which we were not before. E'er I leave this Head, I

beg

Letter V. beg your pardon, SIR, if I take notice to you, that considering the numberless successive Generations that have inhabited this Globe, returning at Death into the common Mass of the same, scattering and mixing with all the other Parts thereof; and joining to this, the incessant river-like Flowing and Transpiration of Matter every moment from the Bodys of Men while they live, as well as their daily Nourishment, Inspiration of Air, and other Additions of Matter to their Bulk: I say, considering these things, it seems to be probable that there is no Particle of Matter on the face of the whole Earth, which has not bin a Part of Man. Nor is this Reasoning confin'd only to our Species, but remains as true of every Order of Animals or Plants, or any other Beings; since they have bin all resolv'd into one another by numberless and ceasless Revolutions, so that nothing is more certain than that every material Thing is all Things, and that all Things are but one.

17. THUS far you allow a constant Motion in Things from sensible

Effects. You say that the Particles of Air, Water, Fire, Æther, Vapors, Exhalations, are without all question in perpetual Motion. You confess the Motion of the imperceptible little Bodys that flow from all greater visible Bodys, which by their Size, Figure, Number, and Motion, operate on our Senses, and produce the several Sensations and Ideas we have of Colors, Tastes, Smells, Heat, Cold, and the like. But you appeal at the same time to my Senses, that *there are some Bodys in absolute Rest, as well as others in absolute Motion*; and you instance Rocks, Iron, Gold, Lead, Timber, and such other things as do not suddenly change their Situation without some external Force. To this I answer, that your Reason, and not your Senses are the true Judges in this case; tho I own that your Senses can never deceive you, if you call your Reason to their Assistance: and to these in consult together I fear not likewise to appeal, as to those very Examples you have alledg'd. But you must always distinguish between the internal Energy, Autokinesy, or essential Action of all Matter, without which it cou'd be capable of

Letter V.

Letter V.

no particular Alteration or Division; and the external local Motion or Changes of Place, which are but the various Modifications of the essential Action as their Subject; the particular Motions being determin'd by other more prevalent Motions, to be direct or circular, fast or slow, continu'd or interrupted, according to the occurrent, subsequent, or circumambient Motions of other Bodys; no part of Matter being without its own internal Energy, however thus determin'd by the neighboring Parts according as their particular Determination is stronger or weaker, yields or resists; and these again continue to be vary'd after some other manner by the next; and so every thing proceeds in endless Changes, that is (as I maintain) in perpetual Motion. Now all the local Motions imaginable being acknowledg'd Accidents, increasing, altering, diminishing, and perishing, without the Destruction of the Subject which they modify, or in which they exist, this Subject cannot be wholly imaginary, a mere abstracted Notion, but something real and positive. Extension cannot be this Subject, since the Idea of Extension does not necessarily

Letter V.

sarily infer any Variety, Alteration, or Motion; and therefore (as I said just now) it must be Action, since all those Motions are but the different Modifications of Action, as all particular Bodys or Quantitys are but the different Modifications of Extension. Of Solidity or Impenetrability I shall put you in mind in its due place, and show how these three essential Attributes or Propertys are inseparable, and do co-operate.

18. BUT not to forget the Appeal to our Senses, wou'd not you believe with the Vulgar that the Stars are no bigger than ordinary Tapers, that the Sun and Moon are no more than a Foot or two in breadth, if your Reason had not computed the Distance between your Eyes and those Bodys, and measur'd their real Bulk by their Appearances in such a distance, with the other proper Arguments which I need not repeat to one that knows 'em so well? Is it not the same thing as to the distinguishing the fixt Stars from the Planets, and understanding the true Motion of the latter, which is very different from what the Senses exhibit? I will not descend so low as a

Letter V. streight Stick appearing crooked in the Water, or the Colors on the Neck of a Dove; nor [?] so high as the Heat, Cold, Relishes, and Odors, that are not in the things themselves, which we denominate from these Sensations. But to come home to the Subject we have in hand; is not local Motion it self sometimes so slow, that it is not perceiv'd by our Senses, no distinguishable Removal from one Point to another, tho the Motion goes constantly on all this while, and that we are convinc'd of it at last by undoubted Effects and visible Intervals, as in the Hand of a Clock or the Shadow of a Dyal? And so it is in Motions that are extremely swift, where no Succession is distinctly observ'd, as in the Passage of a Bullet, or the like. To judg of the Body of a Man or any other Animal by the external Surface, it wou'd seem to have as little internal local Motion (not to speak now of its inseparable Action) as Lead, or Gold, or Stone; nor wou'd we make a different Judgment of any Tree or Plant: And yet unless every Particle of a Tree were in motion, it cou'd neither receive Augmentation when it grows, nor Diminution when it decays. Your Skill in Anatomy, join'd to common Experience, will not let you question but that all the Particles of Animals are in perpetual Motion as well as those of Plants, growing, decaying, transpiring, dissolving, corrupting, becoming fat or lean, hot or cold, tho the Man sits still, or the Beast is asleep, or the Tree stands fixt in its place. The Circulation of the Blood and Sap to every imaginable Part, are now no Secrets in Natural Philosophy. Nor is Iron, Stone, Gold, or Lead, more void of this internal Motion, than those they call fluid Bodys; for otherwise they cou'd never undergo those Alterations, which Air, or Fire, or Water, or any thing else produces in them. But tho by their being reduc'd into these Forms from a precedent different State, tho by their continual wearing, and final Change of Figure, 'tis certain that their Parts are always in motion, yet they are not so easily nor quickly determin'd by other circumambient Motions (tho there are that do it very suddenly) to change their Form or Situation perceptibly to our Senses; which made People imagine that they had no Motion at all, nor any peculiar Determinations.

Letter V.

19. NEVERTHELESS the very remaining of such Bodys in one place is a real Action, the Efforts and Resistance of this Parcel being equal for some time to the determining Motions of the neighboring Bodys that act upon it, and that will not suffer it to pass certain Bounds; which is easily understood from what I have already no less copiously than plainly said of the numberless successive Determinations of Motion, of which this is one kind, and call'd by the People Rest, to distinguish that State of Body from the local Motions that are visible. A Body that descends by Gravity or the stronger Impulse of other Bodys, as its own Impulse is stronger than the Determinations that yield to it on the way, is no less in Action that it is resisted from advancing farther by the yet stronger Resistance of the Earth, and hinder'd from going back by an equal Pressure from the Bodys behind it, than a Ship is without Action, if the Force of the Wind blowing towards the mouth of the River, be equal to that of the Tide flowing towards the Spring of it: for let either of

of these get the better of the other, and the Ship sails. But all this while the Ship was depriv'd only of one sort of Motion, and not of all Effort or Action, no more than Iron, or Lead, or Gold, whose Parts, by their own internal Motion, and by the Motions of the circumambient Bodys, are perpetually growing and increasing, or wearing, moldring, decaying, changing, and perishing in some other manner to us imperceptible; till by the Rust or Tarnish on their Surface, by the Augmentation or Diminution of their Quantity, the Alteration of their Form or Figure, or by some other sensible Effects, we are intirely convinc'd of it at last: Since Rest therefore is but a certain Determination of the Motion of Bodys, a real Action of Resistance between equal Motions, 'tis plain that this is no absolute Inactivity among Bodys, but only a relative Repose with respect to other Bodys that sensibly change their place. Letter V.

20. BUT the Vulgar taking local Motion (as they do all other Relations) for a real Being, have thought Rest a Privation, or that Motion was

Letter V.

Action, and that Rest was a Passion; whereas every Motion is as well a Passion in respect of the Body that gave it the last Determination, as it is an Action compar'd to the Body that it determines next. But the turning of these and such Words from a relative to an absolute Signification, has occasion'd most of the Errors and Disputes on this Subject. However the best Philosophers and Mathematicians, notwithstanding their making Motion extraneous and Rest essential to Matter, have fairly acknowledg'd the actual constant Motion of every Part; being oblig'd to this by the irresistible Evidence of Reason and Experience. They grant that the same incessant Changes and Motions appear in the Bodys under ground, as in those above it; which is confirm'd not only by the nature of the several Beds of Earth in Mines and Quarrys, by the generation of Metals and Minerals, but also by the Appearances of all other subterranean Bodys and Fossils. They own that all the Phænomena of Nature must be explain'd by Motion, by the Action of all things on one another, according to mechanick Principles. And 'tis so in effect that they

they account for all the Diversitys in Nature, for the elementary and sensible Qualitys; for all the Forms, Figures, Mixtures, or other Modifications and Alterations of Matter. Those who think the most truly and nicely therefore on local Motion, consider the Points from which and to which the Body moves, not as in absolute Repose, but only as quiescent with respect to the Motion of that Body: and tho Mr. NEWTON be deem'd an Advocate for extended incorporeal Space, yet he declares[1] that perhaps no one Body is in absolute Rest; that perhaps no[2] immovable bodily Center is to be found in Nature; and in one place he expresses himself in these[3] Words: *The Vulgar attribute Resistance to quiescent, and Impulse to movent Bodys; but Motion and Rest, as commonly conceiv'd, are only respectively*

[1] Fieri enim potest ut nullum re vera quiescat Corpus, ad quod loca motusque referantur. Pag. 7.

[2] Hactenus exposui motus Corporum attractorum ad Centrum immobile, quale tamen vix extat in rerum Natura. Pag. 162.

[3] Vulgus Resistentiam quiescentibus & Impetum moventibus tribuit; sed Motus & Quies, uti vulgo conci-

Letter V. *tively distinguish'd from one another, nor are those things always in true Repose, which are vulgarly consider'd as quiescent.* Thus far that deservedly admir'd Author, who has seen the farthest of all Men living into the actual State of Matter; and indeed all Physicks ought to be denominated from the Title he has given to the first Book of his Principles, viz. *of the Motion of Bodys.*

21. I NEED not ask your pardon, SIR, for being so particular, both because it was your request to me, and for the sake of those who are ignorant of many things which I might suppose to you, and to whom you might nevertheless show my Letter, or speak of my Opinion. I think after all that has bin said, I may now venture to conclude that *Action is essential to Matter,* since it must be the real Subject of all those Modifications which are call'd local Motions, Changes, Differences, or Diversitys; and

---

concipiuntur, respectu solo distinguuntur ab invicem, neque semper vere quiescunt quæ vulgo tanquam quiescentia spectantur. Pag. 2.

princi-

principally because absolute Repose, on which the Inactivity or Lumpishness of Matter was built, is entirely destroy'd, and prov'd no where to exist. This vulgar Error of absolute Rest was occasion'd by the Appearances of heavy, hard, and bulky Bodys; and seeing they did not change that strong Determination (which the People did not conceive to be an Action) but by much stronger Determinations, whose Effects were obvious to their Senses, they concluded first that there was an absolute Rest, and secondly that all Bodys wou'd continue in that State without some foreign Mover, which they imagin'd not to be Matter, since all Bodys were Matter, and that what was natural to the Parts, was so to the Whole. At least, the Philosophers made such Inferences from the Notion of Rest, which they learnt from their Education, and from the sole Judgment of their Senses: for none is born a Divine, Philosopher, or Politician, and therefore every man at the beginning stands on the same ground with the Vulgar, receiving the same Prejudices and Impressions; and however he may extricate himself from many Errors, yet if he leaves any in possession

[redacted]

Letter V. possession unexamin'd, he shall always reason himself into Contradictions or Absurditys from that Principle, tho otherwise justly reckon'd a wise and able Person. Since therefore there is no such absolute Rest in those Examples you have brought, and that on the contrary every other Parcel of Matter, as well as these, are in absolute Motion, you shou'd not side with such Philosophers, as were either the most superstitious or the least perspicacious; nor ought you to argue at all from a vulgar Error: but seeing that every Part of Matter is prov'd to be always in motion, you shou'd conclude that Motion is essential to the Whole, for the same reason that you think Extension to be so; because every Part is extended. To all that will think without Bias, Experience renders these Cases parallel, and Reason evidently demonstrates it.

22. I HAVE industriously omitted to speak any thing of the relative Motions of all those Bodys conceiv'd to be in Repose; and I shall but hint them now, to put you in mind that at the same time they cease not to be absolute. Every thing in the Globe of our Earth (which

(which is as true of all the other Planets) partakes of its constant Motion; for the Motion of the Whole is but the Sum total of the Motion of the Parts; which is not only plain from the Reason of the thing it self, but also from the proportionable Force that is necessary either to impress a new Determination on any Body, or to stop the Determination it has already acquir'd, for the one cannot be less than the other. Tho all the assignable Parts of a Ball in Motion are at rest with respect to one another, or to their places in the Ball; yet none will say, but that they are all in actual Motion as Parts of the Ball, and in relation to every thing without it. So a Passenger shares the Motion of a Ship under Sail, to say nothing of the specific Motions of his human System; tho he's conceiv'd to be at rest, with regard to the place wherein he sits, or to the other Parts of the Ship, which, notwithstanding the Motion of the Whole, keep the same Distance and Position with respect to him. I have likewise dropt but a word (in the fifteenth Paragraph) of the Centripetal Force, by which all the Bodys of the Earth are drawn or

Letter V. tend towards its Center (as all others to the proper Centers of their Motions) nor have I mention'd a syllable of the centrifugal Force, by which they endeavour to recede from the Center in a streight Line, if they are not otherwise determin'd by some stronger Cause: as a Stone whirl'd about in a Sling is detain'd in its Orbit by the Leather, the String of which, being stretcht by the Motion of the Stone, is contracted towards the Stone it self, by its Efforts to fly off directly in every point of the Circle it describes; and at the same time it is equally contracted towards the man's Hand; whence it follows, that the Center approaches as much to the Stone as the Stone does to the Center, which yet does not always happen for many reasons. Notable Effects depend on these Forces the nearer they are to being equal, or the stronger one of 'em is than the other; wherefore the centripetal being much greater than the centrifugal Force of the Parts of the Earth, taking in likewise the Atmosphere, is one main reason that it never loses any of its Matter, and that it always continues of the same Bulk or Dimensions, the centripetal Force of Gravity that detains

tains the several Bodys in their Orbit, being considerably stronger than the centrifugal Force of Motion, by which they strive to fly off in the Tangent. Let the Causes of these Forces be what they will, they are unanswerable Arguments to my purpose of a perpetual Motion in all things. But I shall write no more concerning them, lest I insensibly ingage my self in a Dispute with you about the nature of Gravity, as whether the weight of Bodys be always proportionable to their Quantity of Matter; that is, whether there be more Matter as there is more weight in a cubic Foot of Lead than in a cubic Foot of Cork, which, I know, you maintain after no contemptible Philosophers: or whether the same Quantity of Matter be contain'd in the same Dimensions of Mercury, Gold, Silver, Iron, Lead, Earth, Water, Cork, or Air, tho their specific Gravitys be so different from each other, proceeding partly from external Pressures, and partly from those internal Structures or Modifications which give their common Matter those various Forms that constitute their Species, and are distinguish'd by their Gravity, as they are by their Figures, Co-

Letter V.

Letter V. lors, Tastes, Smells, or any other Affections, arising from their peculiar Disposition, from the Action of other Bodys, or from our Senses and Imagination. This is my own Opinion, whatever be my reasons for it: besides, that were Gravity an essential Attribute, and not a particular Mode of Matter, the same things wou'd equally ponderate in all places and circumstances, as they are every where equally solid or equally extended; nor wou'd they vary in the Retardation or Acceleration of their Descent in various Distances from the Center. With me therefore Gravity infers no Vacuum (as I told you before in the fourteenth Paragraph) and is but one of the many Modes of Action; however this Determination happens, which at present we shall not examine; its real Existence being deny'd by no body, and the Quantitys and Proportions of Motion proceeding from Gravity, or the mutual Action of particular Bodys in this respect, being to be calculated from Fact and Observation, be their physical Causes what you please. For the same reasons I shall pass by the Attraction of the Planets, their gravitating, or acting any other way on one

one another; as 'tis certain not only from the Influence of the Sun, the Tides occasion'd by the Moon, and by several other Arguments, that they very remarkably affect each other, according to their Magnitude, Figure, Distances, and Position.

23. THAT Motion is adventitious to Matter, that it has actually separate and independent Parts, that there is a Void or incorporeal Space, are not the only Mistakes occasion'd by the Notion of absolute Rest. For those Philosophers who were the least superstitious, and who look'd the most narrowly into the Nature of things, have taught that all Matter was animated, as well every Particle of Air, or Water, or Wood, or Iron, or Stone, as a Man, a Brute, or the whole Mass together; being naturally led into this Conceit, because having learnt from others that Matter was essentially inactive (from which Prejudice they did not take care to free themselves) and yet finding by Experience all and every Particle of Matter to be in motion, and believing likewise that Life was different from the organiz'd Body, they concluded that the Cause of this

[redacted]

Letter V.

Motion was some Being intimately join'd to Matter however modify'd, and that it was inseparable from the same. But this pretended Animation is utterly useless, since Matter has Motion of it self, and that there is no real Repose. These enlivening Philosophers were divided into several Classes; so many Expedients are necessary to put some face of Truth upon Error! Some of 'em, as the Stoics, held this Life to be a Soul of the World, coextended with Matter, insinuated and infus'd thro the whole and every part thereof, being it self essentially corporeal, tho infinitely finer than all other Bodys, which, in respect of its Subtilty and Action, were reputed extremely gross: but the universal Soul of the Platonists was immaterial, and a pure Spirit. Others, as STRATO of Lampsacus, and the modern Hylozoicks, thought that the Particles of Matter had Life, and also a degree of Thought, or a direct Perception without any Reflection; to which HERACLITUS of old, and lately SPINOSA, added Understanding or reflex Acts, without ever removing the Difficultys apparently offering themselves against such a precarious Hypothe-

sis,

sis, not as much as showing (tho this Consciousness were granted) how the several reasoning Particles cou'd agree together to form the same Body or System, or to separate or join so regularly on certain occasions, without any jarring or change of Opinions, as to their being better or worse in other places, single or in numerous Company; nor how, tho all the Particles of a Man have Sense and Understanding, he finds but one such Faculty in himself, and that Faculty exerting its Operations only in one place. No less romantic is the plastic Life of other Philosophers, which (according to its modern Reviver, the universally learned Dr. CUDWORTH) is not material, but an inferior sort of Spirit without Sensation or Thought, yet endu'd with a vital Operation and Energy; these Plastics seeming to differ with the Hylozoics only about words, tho pretending a mighty Disagreement, to keep clear, I suppose, of the absurd or invidious Consequences charg'd on their Opinions; as the Jansenists and Calvinists treat one another about Predestination, in which Doctrin they certainly mean the same thing, notwithstanding the nice distinctions of the

Letter V. tend towards its Center (as all others to the proper Centers of their Motions) nor have I mention'd a syllable of the centrifugal Force, by which they endeavour to recede from the Center in a streight Line, if they are not otherwise determin'd by some stronger Cause; as a Stone whirl'd about in a Sling is detain'd in its Orbit by the Leather, the String of which, being stretcht by the Motion of the Stone, is contracted towards the Stone it self, by its Efforts to fly off directly in every point of the Circle it describes; and at the same time it is equally contracted towards the man's Hand; whence it follows, that the Center approaches as much to the Stone as the Stone does to the Center, which yet does not always happen for many reasons. Notable Effects depend on these Forces the nearer they are to being equal, or the stronger one of 'em is than the other; wherefore the centripetal being much greater than the centrifugal Force of the Parts of the Earth, taking in likewise the Atmosphere, is one main reason that it never loses any of its Matter, and that it always continues of the same Bulk or Dimensions, the centripetal Force of Gravity that detains

of great Name and Merit have countenanc'd it by their Approbation, I shall give you the History of this Opinion, as I have done of the rest; tho I might justly neglect it after having prov'd Matter to be essentially active, and that its general Motion was the immediate Subject of all the particular motive Determinations, as Extension is the immediate Subject of the several Figures and Quantitys: for it was likewise to help sluggish Matter to Motion, that this Space (as the room of its Action) was principally devis'd; but Matter not being inactive, nor wanting to have Motion continually imprest by an external Agent, Space may be exterminated from Philosophy, as useless and imaginary. Extension is granted on all hands to be infinite, for it cannot be terminated by Inextension; and the Demonstrations for this are so universally known and acknowledg'd, that I shall not trouble you with repeating them. No less infinite is Matter, when conceiv'd as an extended thing, for you can imagin no bounds of it, to which you may not add more Extension infinitely; and therefore if it be not actually infinite, its Finiteness must proceed

[redacted]

Letter V.

from some other Cause besides its Extension. Those who maintain'd Matter to be finite upon philosophical grounds, imagin'd it to be inactive, divisible into Parts independent and separate, with vacant Interstices; which Parts were heavy or light of themselves, and had various Figures, as well as degrees of Motion, when violently forc'd out of their natural state of Rest. This necessarily led 'em to suppose finite Extensions, at the same time that they allow'd another Extension, which was infinite. And then they cou'd not but make those Extensions essentially different in other respects; the one immovable, impenetrable, indivisible, unchangeable, homogeneal, incorporeal, and all-containing; the other movable, penetrable, divisible, changeable, heterogeneal, corporeal, and contain'd: the one betokening infinite Space, and the other particular Bodys. But this whole Distinction is built on supposing the thing in question, and by the equivocal Signification of the words Place, Whole, Parts, Particles, Divisibility, or the like; and therefore after they took it for granted that Matter was finite, divided into Parts, that it wanted Motion from elsewhere,

and

sis, not as much as showing (tho this Consciousness were granted) how the several reasoning Particles cou'd agree together to form the same Body or System, or to separate or join so regularly on certain occasions, without any jarring or change of Opinions, as to their being better or worse in other places, single or in numerous Company; nor how, tho all the Particles of a Man have Sense and Understanding, he finds but one such Faculty in himself, and that Faculty exerting its Operations only in one place. No less romantic is the plastic Life of other Philosophers, which (according to its modern Reviver, the universally learned Dr. CUDWORTH) is not material, but an inferior sort of Spirit without Sensation or Thought, yet endu'd with a vital Operation and Energy; these Plastics seeming to differ with the Hylozoics only about words, tho pretending a mighty Disagreement, to keep clear, I suppose, of the absurd or invidious Consequences charg'd on their Opinions; as the Jansenists and Calvinists treat one another about Predestination, in which Doctrin they certainly mean the same thing, notwithstanding the nice distinctions of the

Letter V.

P 2 Jansenists

Letter V. Jansenists. But all these Hypotheses are so many visible Shifts to account for the actual Motion of inactive Matter, and to avoid bringing God every moment on the stage, and setting him awork on all occasions, nay in all Actions without distinction, and this too by an absolute and unavoidable Necessity. Thus far of such as provided external or foreign Movers of Matter; and as for those who allow'd it naturally inactive, but assign'd no Cause for its Motion, as ANAXIMANDER, ANAXIMENES, and some other Antients; nor any Cause either of its Motion or Cogitation, as SPINOSA among the Moderns: these, I say, are so unphilosophical as to deserve no further History, and have always afforded matter of Triumph to the Stoics, Spiritualists, and Plastics, or reckon 'em by what other Names or Distributions you may think more proper.

24. BUT the most universal Mistake proceeding from the suppos'd Inactivity of Matter is the Notion of an infinite, extended, and yet incorporeal Space. Because great matters are built on this substantial Space, and that men of

of great Name and Merit have countenanc'd it by their Approbation, I shall give you the History of this Opinion, as I have done of the rest; tho I might justly neglect it after having prov'd Matter to be essentially active, and that its general Motion was the immediate Subject of all the particular motive Determinations, as Extension is the immediate Subject of the several Figures and Quantitys: for it was likewise to help sluggish Matter to Motion, that this Space (as the room of its Action) was principally devis'd; but Matter not being inactive, nor wanting to have Motion continually imprest by an external Agent, Space may be exterminated from Philosophy, as useless and imaginary. Extension is granted on all hands to be infinite, for it cannot be terminated by Inextension; and the Demonstrations for this are so universally known and acknowledg'd, that I shall not trouble you with repeating them. No less infinite is Matter, when conceiv'd as an extended thing, for you can imagin no bounds of it, to which you may not add more Extension infinitely; and therefore if it be not actually infinite, its Finiteness must proceed

Letter V.

from some other Cause besides its Extension. Those who maintain'd Matter to be finite upon philosophical grounds, imagin'd it to be inactive, divisible into Parts independent and separate, with vacant Interstices; which Parts were heavy or light of themselves, and had various Figures, as well as degrees of Motion, when violently forc'd out of their natural state of Rest. This necessarily led 'em to suppose finite Extensions, at the same time that they allow'd another Extension, which was infinite. And then they cou'd not but make those Extensions essentially different in other respects; the one immovable, impenetrable, indivisible, unchangeable, homogeneal, incorporeal, and all-containing; the other movable, penetrable, divisible, changeable, heterogeneal, corporeal, and contain'd: the one betokening infinite Space, and the other particular Bodys. But this whole Distinction is built on supposing the thing in question, and by the equivocal Signification of the words Place, Whole, Parts, Particles, Divisibility, or the like; and therefore after they took it for granted that Matter was finite, divided into Parts, that it wanted Motion from elsewhere, and

and immense, since no finite Quantity, tho never so often repeated, can equal or measure its Extension. Therefore when we say, that Space is all-containing, we mean it of infinite Matter, to distinguish the Whole from the Parts, which yet are not different from the Whole. When we say it permeates all things, we abstract the Extension of Matter from its other Propertys; and so we do, when we say it's incorporeal, not then considering it otherwise than as the Mathematicians in Points, or Lines, or Surfaces. When we affirm it is one, we mean that it is infinite and indivisible; for there's but one Universe, tho there may be numberless Worlds. When we say it is the Place of all things, we signify that it is the Subject of its own Modifications, whether Motions, Figures, or others. When we say it's homogeneal, we mean that Matter is ever the same, be the Modifications of it never so various. And lastly, when we say that finite Bodys cannot exist without an infinite Space, we only say that they cannot be unless they are; for their own Solidity or their Respect to other things is all their Place, abstracting from

[redacted]

Letter V. by God into two equal Spheres; that if they be at a distance from one another, there is between them a measurable Space or Void; or that if they mutually touch in a Point (as perfect Spheres must necessarily do) there is a Space which is not Body, between the other Points of their Circumferences. But is not all this at the same time to suppose Matter finite, to suppose this very Space which they pretend to prove, and from no reason that I can see, but from the bare Consideration of Gravity? I can with Mr. LOCK conceive the Motion of one Body alone without any other succeeding immediately into its place; but it is by abstracting this single Body, and with-holding my Attention from those that really succeed it. I can with him conceive two Bodys at a distance approaching one another, without displacing any thing else till their Superficies come to meet; but 'tis by abstracting from all that they necessarily displace: for, as he judiciously observes himself, it does not follow that any thing exists in such a state, merely because we can conceive it so; or there wou'd be great store of Hydras, Centaurs,

any Consideration of the rest, whereas in reality the Motion of Matter depends on its Solidity and Extension, and so all of 'em inseparably on one another. But the Defenders of Space, after abstracting Extension from Matter, then distinguish'd between Extension in general and the particular Extension of Matter, of this or that Body, as if the latter were something superadded to the former, tho they cou'd not assign the Subject of the former, whether a Substance neither Body nor Spirit, or a new kind of Nothing endow'd with the Propertys of a Being. Nay many of them have not stuck to make it pass for the Supreme Being it self, or at least for an inadequate Conception of God, as may be seen in the ingenious Mr. RALPHSON's Book of Real Space, to whom I had an eye in the two foregoing Paragraphs; tho, as may be likewise learnt from his own Authoritys, he was neither the first Broacher of this Conceit, nor the only Maintainer of it now. I am satisfy'd that most of those Gentlemen did firmly believe the Existence of a Deity, and I charitably hope it of 'em all; but in my Opinion their unwary Zeal refin'd him into

mere

[redacted]

Letter V. confuted; not to insist on insurmountable Difficultys arising from those fictitious Extremitys, as to their Consistence, Figure, whether any thing can break loose from them, what becomes of such Fractions, and a thousand other Riddles. I can further gratify him in the Consideration of divided Particles; but I deny that the Continuity of infinite Matter can ever be separated by any distinct Surfaces with void intermediate Spaces; for we only abstract (as I told you in the sixth and seventh Paragraphs) what we call Parts, considering by it self so much of Extension as is for our purpose, and distinguishing such Parcels not by real Divisions from the Whole, but by the Modifications of Color, Figure, Motion, or the like, as we consider the Heat without the Light of the Sun. He says further, That *those who assert the Impossibility of Space existing without Matter, must not only make Body infinite, but must also deny a power in God to annihilate any part of Matter.* That they make Matter infinite is confest; but what he adds about Annihilation is deny'd: for besides that no Revelation from God can be produc'd, wherein he has

has declar'd that he will annihilate any part of Matter, so it is no Argument for a real Space, that God has it in his power to annihilate, no more than that the World shall actually finish in three Days, because I conceive it possible for God to destroy it in that short time. I know no reason (of what he asserts in the same place) why the Maintainers of infinite Matter shou'd *be loth to speak out their opinion*, any more than the Maintainers of infinite Space, or of any other Infinite, for the word is apply'd to more Subjects than one or two: and what made CARTESIUS backward to affirm expresly that Matter was infinite, contenting himself with the word Indefinite, was his being sure on the one hand that Extension was infinite; and yet, allowing withal that Matter was naturally inactive and really divisible, he cou'd not well demonstrate its Infinity, tho you that read him so often need no Proofs that he sometimes positively affirm'd it. As for the Theological Exceptions to this Position, they are of little weight, and show the Philosophy of some Men to be as little as their Zeal is great and fervent; nor do I believe that the moderate and

Letter V.

Letter V. by God into two equal Spheres; that if they be at a distance from one another, there is between them a measurable Space or Void; or that if they mutually touch in a Point (as perfect Spheres must necessarily do) there is a Space which is not Body, between the other Points of their Circumferences. But is not all this at the same time to suppose Matter finite, to suppose this very Space which they pretend to prove, and from no reason that I can see, but from the bare Consideration of Gravity? I can with Mr. LOCK conceive the Motion of one Body alone without any other succeeding immediately into its place; but it is by abstracting this single Body, and with-holding my Attention from those that really succeed it. I can with him conceive two Bodys at a distance approaching one another, without displacing any thing else till their Superficies come to meet; but 'tis by abstracting from all that they necessarily displace: for, as he judiciously observes himself, it does not follow that any thing exists in such a state, merely because we can conceive it so; or there wou'd be great store of Hydras, Centaurs,

tho never so able; not that we know it the less for all this, but on the contrary because we know it better than any thing which is capable of a Definition. Simple Ideas, such as Motion, Extension, Color, Sound, are self-evident, and their Names by no means definable; but the single Words which denote complex Ideas, that is, a Collection of self-evident Ideas consider'd as one thing, are the true Objects of Definition; because the several Terms for those Ideas, when put together, show the Connection, Possibility, and Conception of the Whole. Thus all the Words in the world cou'd not explain Blue, nor give the clear Idea of it to one who never saw that Color; but supposing the same Person never saw any Gold, tho well acquainted with other Metals, yet he'll be able to form a distinct Notion of it, from the mouth of another who describes it of a certain Yellowness and Weight, malleable, fusible, fixt, and the like. When the Names therefore of simple Ideas are defin'd, we must not imagine it to be their Subjects; for synonymous Terms do not explain the nature of the thing, but give us the meaning of the Word in more intelligible

Letter V. confuted; not to insist on insurmountable Difficultys arising from those fictitious Extremitys, as to their Consistence, Figure, whether any thing can break loose from them, what becomes of such Fractions, and a thousand other Riddles. I can further gratify him in the Consideration of divided Particles; but I deny that the Continuity of infinite Matter can ever be separated by any distinct Surfaces with void intermediate Spaces; for we only abstract (as I told you in the sixth and seventh Paragraphs) what we call Parts, considering by it self so much of Extension as is for our purpose, and distinguishing such Parcels not by real Divisions from the Whole, but by the Modifications of Color, Figure, Motion, or the like, as we consider the Heat without the Light of the Sun. He says further, That *those who assert the Impossibility of Space existing without Matter, must not only make Body infinite, but must also deny a power in God to annihilate any part of Matter.* That they make Matter infinite is confest; but what he adds about Annihilation is deny'd: for besides that no Revelation from God can be produc'd, wherein he

has

has declar'd that he will annihilate any part of Matter, so it is no Argument for a real Space, that God has it in his power to annihilate, no more than that the World shall actually finish in three Days, because I conceive it possible for God to destroy it in that short time. I know no reason (of what he asserts in the same place) why the Maintainers of infinite Matter shou'd *be loth to speak out their opinion*, any more than the Maintainers of infinite Space, or of any other Infinite, for the word is apply'd to more Subjects than one or two: and what made CARTESIUS backward to affirm expresly that Matter was infinite, contenting himself with the word Indefinite, was his being sure on the one hand that Extension was infinite; and yet, allowing withal that Matter was naturally inactive and really divisible, he cou'd not well demonstrate its Infinity, tho you that read him so often need no Proofs that he sometimes positively affirm'd it. As for the Theological Exceptions to this Position, they are of little weight, and show the Philosophy of some Men to be as little as their Zeal is great and fervent; nor do I believe that the moderate and

Letter V.

Matter those Attributes are never otherwise but mentally divided from one another. That Extension, for example, exhausts the Idea of Matter, I deny; since it does not imply Solidity or Motion: but that all extended is Matter, may be very true, tho Matter be not barely extended, but likewise active and solid. But tho in the pure Consideration of those Ideas the one does not suppose the other, and that each of 'em has certain Modes which are conceiv'd to belong immediately to it self, yet they are so firmly linkt in Nature, that the one cannot exist without the other, and they all necessarily concur to the producing of those Modes which are proper to each. Extension is the immediate Subject of all the Divisions, Figures, and Parcels of Matter; but 'tis Action that causes those Alterations, and they cou'd not be distinct without Solidity. Action is the immediate Cause of all local Motions, Changes, or Varietys in Matter; but Extension is the Subject and Measure of their Distances: and tho upon Solidity depends the Resistance, Impulse, and Protrusion of Bodys, yet 'tis Action that produces them in Extension. Solidity, Extension, and Action, are therefore three distinct Ideas, but not three different things; only the various Considerations of one and the self-same Matter. To return to our particular Subject, you may easily perceive by this time, that the *Vis motrix*, the true motive Force is this essential Action of Matter; and that the *Vis impressa*, the imprest Force of particular Bodys, is some Determination of the general Action: for in this sense it's indisputable that nothing can move, that is, determine it self, till it be determin'd by some other thing: so that Matter being active, the Direction given to that Action in any part, wou'd of it self for ever continue, because no Effect can be without a Cause, and by consequence this Direction must be chang'd by some greater Force, as that by another, and so on, one never ending but for another to begin, no more than any Figure is destroy'd in Matter, but to make place for another. Thus one Motion is always succeeded by another Motion, and never by absolute Rest, no more than in any Parcel of Matter the ceasing of one Figure is the ceasing of all, which is impossible. These Determinations of Motion in the Parts of solid extended Matter, are what we call the Phaeno-

Letter V.

Terms: wherefore Passage, Translation, Removing, successive Application, are but other words for Motion, and no Definitions of the thing, no more than ARISTOTLE's *Act of a being in power so far forth as it is in power*; but all particular local Motions may be defin'd by the Lines they describe, and the Causes that determine the Course or Degrees of their Motion. The same is to be understood of the general Extension of Matter, and of its particular Determinations, by Measure, Figures, or any other way. The Solidity of all Matter is likewise an intuitive or undefinable Idea. But I do not here understand Solidity in the sense of Geometers, of every assign'd Quantity that has three Dimensions; but as Mr. LOCK has substituted this positive Term, instead of the negative one of Impenetrability, for the Resistance we find in every Body to the Entrance of any other Body into the place it possesses till it has left it: as a drop of Water equally prest on all sides, is an insurmountable Obstacle for the strongest Bodys in the Universe to join, till it be remov'd; and so a piece of Wood will keep your two Hands from ever coming together, tho you endea-

Anatomy, will be convinc'd that all the Motions of sitting, standing, lying, rising, running, walking, and such others, have their proper, external, material, and proportionable Determinations. After Mr. NEWTON, in the Preface of his *Mathematical Principles of Natural Philosophy*, has spoken of Gravity, Elasticity, Resistance, Impulse, and Attraction, and of his Explication of the mundane Systm by these Principles; * *I wish*, adds he, *that we cou'd by the same Method of reasoning be able to explain the other Phænomena of Nature from mechanic Principles! for I am induc'd by divers Considerations to suspect a little, that all these may depend on certain Forces, whereby from Causes yet undiscover'd the Particles of Bodys are mutually impell'd against each other, and cohere according to regular Figures, or whereby they recede and are driven from one another: which*

* Utinam cætera Naturæ Phænomena ex Principiis mechanicis eodem argumentandi genere derivare liceret! Nam multa me movent, ut nonnihil suspicer ea omnia ex viribus quibusdam pendere posse, quibus Corporum particulæ per causas nondum cognitas vel in se mutuo impelluntur & secundum Figuras regulares cohærent, vel ab invicem fugantur & recedunt: quibus viribus ignotis, Philosophi hactenus Naturam frustra tentarunt.

Forces

Letter V. Matter those Attributes are never otherwise but mentally divided from one another. That Extension, for example, exhausts the Idea of Matter, I deny; since it does not imply Solidity or Motion: but that all extended is Matter, may be very true, tho Matter be not barely extended, but likewise active and solid. But tho in the pure Consideration of those Ideas the one does not suppose the other, and that each of 'em has certain Modes which are conceiv'd to belong immediately to it self, yet they are so firmly linkt in Nature, that the one cannot exist without the other, and they all necessarily concur to the producing of those Modes which are proper to each. Extension is the immediate Subject of all the Divisions, Figures, and Parcels of Matter; but 'tis Action that causes those Alterations, and they cou'd not be distinct without Solidity. Action is the immediate Cause of all local Motions, Changes, or Varietys in Matter; but Extension is the Subject and Measure of their Distances: and tho upon Solidity depends the Resistance, Impulse, and Protrusion of Bodys, yet 'tis Action that produces them in Extension. Solidity, Extension, and Action, are therefore

three

three distinct Ideas, but not three different things; only the various Considerations of one and the self-same Matter. To return to our particular Subject, you may easily perceive by this time, that the *Vis motrix*, the true motive Force is this essential Action of Matter; and that the *Vis impressa*, the imprest Force of particular Bodys, is some Determination of the general Action: for in this sense it's indisputable that nothing can move, that is, determine it self, till it be determin'd by some other thing: so that Matter being active, the Direction given to that Action in any part, wou'd of it self for ever continue, because no Effect can be without a Cause, and by consequence this Direction must be chang'd by some greater Force, as that by another, and so on, one never ending but for another to begin, no more than any Figure is destroy'd in Matter, but to make place for another. Thus one Motion is always succeeded by another Motion, and never by absolute Rest, no more than in any Parcel of Matter the ceasing of one Figure is the ceasing of all, which is impossible. These Determinations of Motion in the Parts of solid extended Matter, are what we call the Phænomena

Letter V. mena of Nature, and to which we give Names or ascribe Uses, Perfection or Imperfection, according as they affect our Senses, and cause Pain or Pleasure to our Bodys, contribute to our Preservation or Destruction: but we do not always denominate 'em from their real Causes, or ways of producing one another, as the Elasticity, Hardness, Softness, Fluidity, Quantity, Figures, and Relations of particular Bodys. On the contrary we frequently attribute many Determinations of Motion to no Cause at all, as the spontaneous Motion of Animals: for, however those Motions may be accompany'd by Thought, yet, consider'd as Motions, they have their physical Causes, as a Dog's running after a Hare, the Bulk of the external Object acting by its whole Force of Impulse or Attraction on the Nerves, which are so dispos'd with the Muscles, Joints, and other Parts, as to produce various Motions in the Animal Machine. And whoever understands in any measure the Action of Bodys on one another by their immediate Contact, or by the imperceptible Particles that continually flow from them, and to this Knowledg joins that of Mechanics, Hydrostatics, and

Anatomy,

Anatomy, will be convinc'd that all the Motions of sitting, standing, lying, rising, running, walking, and such others, have their proper, external, material, and proportionable Determinations. After Mr. NEWTON, in the Preface of his *Mathematical Principles of Natural Philosophy*, has spoken of Gravity, Elasticity, Resistance, Impulse, and Attraction, and of his Explication of the mundane System by these Principles; * *I wish*, adds he, *that we cou'd by the same Method of reasoning be able to explain the other Phænomena of Nature from mechanic Principles! for I am induc'd by divers Considerations to suspect a little, that all these may depend on certain Forces, whereby from Causes yet undiscover'd the Particles of Bodys are mutually impell'd against each other, and cohere according to regular Figures, or whereby they recede and are driven from one another: which*

* Utinam cætera Naturæ Phænomena ex Principiis mechanicis eodem argumentandi genere derivare liceret! Nam multa me movent, ut nonnihil suspicer ea omnia ex viribus quibusdam pendere posse, quibus Corporum particulæ per causas nondum cognitas vel in se mutuo impelluntur & secundum Figuras regulares cohærent, vel ab invicem fugantur & recedunt: quibus viribus ignotis, Philosophi hactenus Naturam frustra tentarunt.

Forces

Letter V. Philosophy may be made of this essential Motion of Matter, besides a clearer Knowledg of Nature in general, and the particular Decision of the Controversys about the moving Force, about local Motion without or with a Void, about the nature of Space, and the Infinity of Matter. I am confident that before your reading thus far, you have already made the Application of this Doctrin to several other Difficultys, having impartially revolv'd in your own Mind the unsatisfactory Guesses and miserable Circles, rather than genuine Explications of the Schools; and that you have consider'd likewise what numberless Errors may branch themselves over the whole Body of Philosophy, from any one false Principle laid down for undisputed Truth, without Proof or Examination. What Observations of this kind I have made my self from time to time, I shall freely impart to you and our common Friend, who alone philosophizes at Court, and who exceeds all the rest in Politeness and Address, as much as he does in Wisdom and Literature, his superior Genius and admirable Sense no less distinguishing him in ordinary

one Property as well as the other, and that no reason can be assign'd why he shou'd not endue it with the former as well as with the latter; is there likewise no necessity that he shou'd ever or rather always direct its Motions? Can the Formation of Animals or Plants be accounted for from the Action, any more than from the Extension of Matter? Or are you able to imagine that the Action and Reaction of Bodys, of all the Particles of Matter on one another, cou'd ever have the Contrivance to make any one of those admirable vegetable or animal Machines? All your Skill in Mechanism can no more help you, than it did CARTESIUS, to find out Rules and Engines for making either a Man or a Mouse. All the jumbling of Atoms, all the Chances you can suppose for it, cou'd no more bring the Parts of the Universe into their present Order, nor continue them in the same, nor cause the Organization of a Flower or a Fly, than you can imagine that by tumbling together the Letters of a Printer a million of times, they shou'd ever fall at last into such a Position, as to make the *Æneis* of VIRGIL, or the *Ilias* of

Letter V.

HOMER, or any other Book in the world. And as for the Infinity of Matter, it only excludes, what all reasonable and good Men must exclude, an extended corporeal God, but not a pure Spirit or immaterial Being. I am persuaded, that in omitting many other common Objections, you purposely spar'd me, knowing there was no end of Absurditys from false or precarious Systems; Absurditys so monstrous, that they have driven several of the Cartesians (to name no others) to as monstrous Hypotheses, when not knowing wherein consisted the moving Force, and for avoiding the Transition of Accidents from one Subject to another, they are not asham'd to say, that God takes the Motion from one Bowl that is running forward (for example) and communicates it to the other against which it rubs, continuing it during its Course by his immediate Concurrence, and taking it away by such degrees as are observ'd in the ordinary Laws of Motion. Is this to explain any thing? Or are these the men that laugh at Sympathy, Antipathy, occult Qualitys, or the like? I know to whom I address my self, when I speak of every

thing

thing so succinctly; any the least Hint being enough for you, to work out all the rest by your own most happy Genius: besides that the ordinary Solutions can never satisfy any man who denies the ordinary Suppositions.

Letter V.

31. PRAY, against your writing to me next, be pleas'd to consider whether the Mathematicians (who are generally the best and strictest Reasoners, tho they build sometimes on groundless Suppositions, and have often made real Beings of abstracted Ideas) whether, I say, they did not perceive, without reflecting that they did so, the Necessity of this intrinsick and essential Action of Matter, by their *Conatus ad Motum?* I have purposely omitted insisting on this, when I show'd you that it was the Discovery of the same perpetual and universal Action, that gave a Being to the Systems of the Stoics, Plastics, Hylozoics, and others: for my Intention has not bin to write all I cou'd say on this Subject, but as much as I thought necessary to answer your Objections, and to bring you over to the same Opinion. Neither will I point out to you what further use in Philosophy

Letter V. Philosophy may be made of this essential Motion of Matter, besides a clearer Knowledg of Nature in general, and the particular Decision of the Controversys about the moving Force, about local Motion without or with a Void, about the nature of Space, and the Infinity of Matter. I am confident that before your reading thus far, you have already made the Application of this Doctrin to several other Difficultys, having impartially revolv'd in your own Mind the unsatisfactory Guesses and miserable Circles, rather than genuine Explications of the Schools; and that you have consider'd likewise what numberless Errors may branch themselves over the whole Body of Philosophy, from any one false Principle laid down for undisputed Truth, without Proof or Examination. What Observations of this kind I have made my self from time to time, I shall freely impart to you and our common Friend, who alone philosophizes at Court, and who exceeds all the rest in Politeness and Address, as much as he does in Wisdom and Literature, his superior Genius and admirable Sense no less distinguishing him in ordinary

ordinary Ceremonys, than in the nicest and most arduous Points of State Affairs. But I shall give you no further trouble, SIR, till you are next dispos'd to honor me with your Commands. Letter V.

FINIS.